ADVANCED LISTENING COMPREHENSION

Developing Aural and Notetaking Skills

Second Edition

Patricia A. Dunkel
Frank Pialorsi
Joann Kozyrev

Heinle & Heinle Publishers

I(T)P   An International Thomson Publishing Company

Pacific Grove • Albany • Bonn • Boston • Cincinnati • Detroit • London • Madrid • Melbourne
Mexico City • New York • Paris • San Francisco • Tokyo • Toronto • Washington

The publication of *Advanced Listening Comprehension, Second Edition* was directed by the members of the Newbury House Publishing Team at Heinle & Heinle.

Erik Gundersen, Editorial Director
John F. McHugh, Market Development Director
Kristin Thalheimer, Production Services Coordinator

Also participating in the publication of this program were:

Publisher: Stanley J. Galek
Director of Production: Elizabeth Holthaus
Project Manager: Angela Malovich Castro, English Language Trainers
Senior Assistant Editor: Ken Pratt
Manufacturing Coordinator: Mary Beth Hennebury
Interior Designer: Carol H. Rose
Illustrator: Kevin Flynn
Photo Researcher: Philippe Heckly
Photo/Video Specialist: Jonathan Stark
Cover Designer: Gina Petti, Rotunda Design

Library   of   Congress   Cataloging-in-Pulication   Data

Dunkel, Patricia
        Advanced listening comprehension / Patricia Dunkel, Frank Pialorsi,
    Joann Kozyrez. -- 2nd ed.
            p.   cm.
        Includes bibliographical references.
        Summary: Introduces the fundamentals of listening and note-taking
    using written excercises and audio activities.
        ISBN 0-8384-4842-9
        1. English language--Textbooks for foreign speakers.
    2. Listening.   [1. English language--Textbooks for foreign speakers.
    2. Listening.   3. Note-taking.]   I. Pialorsi, Frank.   II. Kozyrez, Joann.   III. Title.
    PE1128. D827 1995
        428.3'4--dc20

                                                                    95-26669
                                                                    CIP
                                                                    AC

Heinle & Heinle Publishers is a division of International Thomson Publishing, Inc.

Manufactured in the United States of America.

ISBN 0-8384-4842-9

10 9 8 7 6 5 4 3 2 1

CONTENTS

TO THE TEACHER

Advanced Listening Comprehension, Second Edition is a complete listening and notetaking skills program for advanced level students of English as a second or foreign language. Lectures and readings on topics of universal interest like *The Great Flood of 1993, Gender & Communication,* and *The Egyptian Pyramids* provide stimulating, content-based springboards for developing comprehension, notetaking, and academic study skills.

Advanced Listening Comprehension, Second Edition is one in a series of listening comprehension publications. The complete program has been designed to meet the needs of students from the beginning to the advanced levels and includes the following:

- *Start with Listening* .... beginning
- *Intermediate Listening Comprehension* .... intermediate
- *Advanced Listening Comprehension* .... advanced

Pedagogical Overview

I. Focus on Developing Academic Listening Comprehension Proficiency: Models of Noninteractive and Interactive Lectures

The lecture method of instruction pervades institutions of higher learning in North America and in many areas throughout the world. It is considered to be a cost/effective method of instruction and "the most dramatic way of presenting to the largest number of students a critical distillation of ideas and information on a subject in the short possible time" (Elsen, cited in Gage and Berliner, 1984, p. 454). Not only do many students encounter the lecture method of instruction during university life, but more and more students across the globe are experiencing lectures given in English. As Flowerdew (1994) observes, as a result of the spread of English as an international language, increasing numbers of people are studying at university level through the medium of English, whether in their own country or in English-speaking countries as international students. He notes, further, that a major part of the university experience of these domestic and international students involves listening to lectures and developing academic listening skills.

"Academic listening skills are thus an essential component of communicative competence in a university setting" (Flowerdew, 1994, p. 7).

Richards (1983), Rost (1990), and Flowerdew (1994) have contributed a substantial amount of knowledge to the growing body of literature on what constitutes and fosters proficiency in academic listening, as well as conversational listening. In his scholarly book *Academic Listening: Research Perspectives*, Flowerdew, for example, identifies a number of the distinctive features of academic listening, pointing out that one of the most significant features that distinguishes academic listening from conversational listening is the lack (or relatively rare use) of turn-taking in academic listening. "In conversation, turn-taking is obviously essential, while in lectures turn-taking conventions will only be required if questions are allowed from the audience or come from the lecturer" (p. 11). As a result, the lecture listener may have to listen with concentration for long stretches of time without having the chance to take a turn to speak during the lecture presentation. In other words, the listener must develop the ability "to concentrate on and understand long stretches of talk without the opportunity of engaging in the facilitating functions of interactive discourse, such as asking for repetition, negotiating meaning, using repair strategies, etc." (Flowerdew, 1994, p. 11). Some lecture situations allow for little or no participation and interaction from the student-listener. This type of lecture is sometimes referred to as a "talk-and-chalk" or a noninteractive lecture. In the United States, students typically experience this type of lecture when attending classes held in large lecture halls containing large numbers of students, although the nonparticipatory lecture can (and often does) occur in nearly every instructional setting.

The noninteractive lecture situation is, however, not the only type of lecture experience that international students may have at a university where English is the only or dominant language of instruction. Some lecturers do adopt a more **interactive** lecturing style, particularly when they are lecturing to relatively small audiences, i. e., of thirty or fewer students. The language of the more interactive lecturer requires that students engage in more conversational listening, and the language of the lecturer will generally contain some of the hallmarks and conventions of conversation, albeit of academic conversation. The lecturer, for example, may make allowance for (or encourage) questions from listeners seeking clarification of information heard or read in a reading assignment, or the lecturer may ask questions to check that the listeners understood bits of information and points made.

Advanced Listening Comprehension, 2nd edition offers students models of both kinds of lectures: the noninteractive academic lecture and the slightly more interactive academic lecture. In addition, a third, more informal style of information presentation is offered. *Advanced Listening Comprehension, 2nd edition* listeners are presented with three models of lecture discourse on the same topic. The first model exposes students to uninterrupted lecture discourse, similar to the kind heard in a large-audience, noninteractive "talk-and-chalk" lecture, or to a news broadcast heard on the radio. During this initial listening, the student listens to perceive or become familiar with the overall general structure and content of the lecture. While listening, the learner reviews a notetaking outline of the lecture, which outlines aspects of the content and structure of the information. With this initial listening experience, the listener is "oriented" toward the structure and content of the lecture, and he or she absorbs some background needed to support a more thorough understanding of the lecture. The second lecture presentation models a more slow-paced delivery of information; the lecture is interrupted by a mentor-guide who asks questions of the listener/notetaker and who attempts to assist with the task of taking notes on the lecture information. (The mentor highlights some of the main ideas, and reiterates many of the details so the listener can decide whether or not to encode the information in his or her notes.) The third exemplar models a more conversational style (albeit a more academic conversational style), with the speaker (a peer) paraphrasing and restructuring the information presented during the first and second lectures. The language includes occasional hesitations, repairs, and verbal fillers in the speech.

II. Focus on Developing Notetaking Skills: Providing Opportunity to Develop the Ability to Select and Encode Information in Notes

In addition to contrasting the difference in turn-taking conventions associated with academic and conversational styles discussed previously, Flowerdew (1994) points out that conversational and academic listening differ one from the other in terms of the listener's desire to take notes on the information heard. To do so, the listener needs to engage in a five-stage process: he or she must "decode, comprehend, identify main points, decide when to record these, write quickly and clearly" (Flowerdew, 1994, p. 11). Lecture notes are usually taken and stored in notebooks for study-and-review purposes. In their article entitled "Second Language Listening Comprehension and Lecture Note-taking," Chaudron, Loschky, and Cook (1995) underscore the importance of this **external storage function** of lecture notes. The structure and format of *Advanced Listening Comprehension, 2nd edition* reinforces the importance of this **external storage function** of the notes taken since the students must use the notes taken during the lectures to respond to short-answer and mini-essay examination questions given several class sessions following delivery of the lecture. *Advanced Listening Comprehension, 2nd edition* also gives students the chance to develop their individual notetaking approaches and styles, though it provides some guidance in the form of the notetaking mentor who interrupts the lecture to provide students with additional time to write down information, to fill in information missed, and to signal some of the major global ideas and details contained in the information heard.

III. Focus on Developing General Communication Skills: Broadening the Base of Skill Development

Although development of academic listening comprehension proficiency and notetaking skill are chief objectives of the instructional program of *Advanced Listening Comprehension, 2nd edition*, they are not the exclusive goals of the program. The authors recognize that advanced ESL students are not just "information sponges." They are much more than that. In addition to obtaining and absorbing information and knowledge, they also function as users and creators of information and knowledge. Furthermore, they react to information learned, often in discussion of issues with peers. In addition, during their university days, students not only *listen* to obtain and learn information, they also *read* to acquire information, and they discuss and react to the information gained via both their ears and eyes. Occasionally, they are expected to give oral reports in class and to participate in study groups (see Mason, 1994). Upon occasion, they are required to interact after class with their instructors, or if they are teaching assistants, to interact with their students. They commonly interact with their peers. A student might, for example, be asked by a peer who was absent from a lecture class to provide him or her with a synopsis of the lecture missed or a summary of the reading assignment given by the professor. The students might also be asked to evaluate or to react to the information presented. *Advanced Listening Comprehension, 2nd edition* seeks, therefore, to help students not only grasp, comprehend, and store information they have heard and read, but also to construct and share information through speaking and writing. It provides students an opportunity to read information related to (but not precisely the same as) the topics of the lectures, and it requires the learner to discuss issues in oral exchanges and/or written communication.

IV. Summary Goals

In brief, the goals of *Advanced Listening Comprehension, 2nd edition* are primarily threefold: (1) to help students build their academic listening comprehension proficiency in English; (2) to assist them in developing or improving their English-lecture notetaking skills; and (3) to enhance their ability to read and discuss information and issues related to the general and/or specific topics contained in the lectures heard. These goals are achieved, we trust, with the aid of the instructional design of the units and the eclectic approach outlined below.

The Instructional Design of Each Unit

    I.   **Chapter 1**

        A. Proverbs and Wise Sayings: Students read proverbs and sayings to ponder and/or discuss general and specific meanings, as well as relevance.

        B. Prelistening: Students read a short introduction to and synopsis of the focus and content of the information contained in the discourse.

        C. Think About This: Students answer one or two questions to anticipate content and to share experiences and feelings evoked by the questions.

        D. Types of Information Presentations and Delivery Styles: Students listen to three models of the discourse on the topic with different task requirements for each model.

1. *The Orientation Listening Model*—Students get oriented to the structure and content of the lecture and build background knowledge (the discourse is scripted and representative of broadcast style).

2. *The Listening & Notetaking Model*—Students listen to the lecture with mentoring support for notetaking (the lecture is scripted with elements of redundancy provided and is given at a slightly slower speed than that of the Orientation Listening).

3. *Listening to a Recounting of the Lecture*—Students listen to a recounting of the lecture by a fellow student and native speaker of English (the lecture is presented as recalled by a student-listener; the notes taken by the listener can be checked for accuracy and completeness during the presentation; the style includes characteristics of more extemporaneous presentations, including use of redundancies, paraphrases, verbal fillers (e.g., "uhmmm," "errr") repetitions, corrections, and so forth in the speech).

E. **Recapping the Lecture From the Notes Taken:** Students recap the lecture from the notes they took.

F. **Reading Expansion:** Students read authentic material (e. g., a newspaper article, a segment of a book, a research report, and so forth) on a related topic.

1. Students read a textbook-type passage on the subject and/or
2. Students read an authentic text other than a textbook on the subject (e.g., a newspaper report, a letter, a poem, and so forth).

G. **Conversing With a Partner About the Issues:** Students discuss and react to the issues by responding to questions related to the topic.

H. **Journal Writing:** Students maintain a written journal in which they write about topics and issues of interest or concern to them.

II. **Chapter 2** (The above structure is repeated with a related lecture topic.)

III. **Unit Exam: Information Recognition/Recall Exam**—Students answer limited-response questions (fill-in-the-blank and short-answer questions) and essay-type questions using the notes they took on the lecture. The storage function of the notes is emphasized in this component of the listening and notetaking program. Students are also asked to construct a number of test questions to give fellow students and peers. Students, thus, participate in test construction and information checking in individual ways.

References

Chaudron, C., Loschky, L., & Cook, J. (1994). Second language listening comprehension and lecture note-taking (pp. 75–92). In J. Flowerdew's (Ed.) *Academic Listening: Research Perspectives.* New York: Cambridge University Press.

Flowerdew, J. (Ed.) (1994). *Academic Listening: Research Perspectives*. New York: Cambridge University Press.

Gage, N. L., & Berliner, D. C. (1984). *Educational Psychology* (3rd ed.) Boston: Houghton Mifflin.

Mason, A. (1994). By dint of: Student and lecturer perceptions of lecture comprehension strategies in first-term graduate study (pp. 199–218). In J. Flowerdew's (Ed.). *Academic Listening: Research Perspectives*. New York: Cambridge University Press.

Richards, J. (1983). Listening comprehension: Approach, design, procedure. *TESOL Quarterly, 17*. 219–40.

Rost, M. (1990). *Listening in Language Learning*. New York: Longman.

UNIT ONE

History:
The Passing of Time
and Civilizations

Think about and discuss the meaning of the following quotation:

"Those who cannot remember the past are condemned to repeat it."

—George Santayana (1863–1952)
American philosopher and poet

CHAPTER 1

THE END OF AN EMPIRE
Montezuma and Cortes

Think about and discuss the meaning of the following quotations:

"Veni. Vidi. Vici." (I came. I saw. I conquered.)
—Julius Caesar (100–44 B.C.)
"I came. I saw. God conquered."
—Charles V (1500–1558)

". . .God has purposely allowed these lands (Mexico) to be discovered . . . causing these barbaric tribes to be enlightened and brought to the faith.' (First Dispatch, July 10, 1519 to Charles V)
"The Aztecs said that by no means would they give themselves up, for as long as one of them was left he would die fighting, and that we would get nothing of theirs because they would burn everything or throw it into the water." (Third Dispatch, May 15, 1522 to Charles V)
—Hernan Cortes (1485–1547)

A. Pre-listening Activities

Preview of the Content

The Aztec Empire of Mexico was one of the most powerful, culturally advanced empires in the fifteenth and sixteenth centuries. And yet, in slightly less than two years, this mighty empire was conquered by a small band of treasure-seeking Spanish adventurers. Why did this happen? What factors entered into the downfall of this mighty empire and led to the destruction of such a sophisticated New World culture? In a few minutes, we'll take a look at some of the most obvious factors that led to the fall of the great empire of Montezuma.

Think about this

Think of several events you consider to be major turning points in the history of your country. Why were these events turning points? Share your information with a partner.

B. Input Models and Listening Activities

Orientation Listening

As you listen to the lecture for the first time, use the outline below to help you understand the general content of the lecture and the topics discussed. The outline should help you perceive the overall structure of the lecture and the main ideas presented by the lecturer.

I. Extent and power of the Aztec empire
   A. Subjugations of area Indians
   B. Extension of empire from Mexico City to Guatemala
   C. Human sacrifices to Aztec gods
   D. Aztec capital of Tenochtitlan
      1. Largest city in sixteenth century
      2. Military fortress
      3. Effective military intelligence system

II. Conquest of Aztec empire
   A. Forewarning of Spanish invasion
      1. Appearance of white, bearded men
      2. Legend of Aztec god Quetzalcoatl
      3. Cortes thought to be Quetzalcoatl by Montezuma
      4. Spanish gathering of Indian allies
   B. Defeat of the Aztecs
      1. Invasion of the city and capture of the king
      2. Aztec rebellion against the conquerors
      3. Death of Montezuma
      4. Destruction of the capital
      5. Slaughter of the Indians

III. Factors in the downfall of the Aztecs
   A. Fear of the supernatural
   B. Role of La Malinche, the Indian woman
   C. Cortes's use of Indian allies
   D. Spaniards' superior weaponry
   E. Spaniards' greed

IV. Fusion of Indian and European cultures creating the Republic of Mexico

Listening and Notetaking

Now that you've listened to the lecture once, listen to it again and take notes. The lecturer will present a slower-paced version of the lecture and will reiterate information so you will have time to take notes. You will be assisted in your notetaking by a notetaking mentor, who will ask you to check that you wrote down important information.

_____

_____

_____

_____

_____

_____

_____

_____

_____

_____

_____

_____

_____

_____

_____

_____

_____

_____

_____

_____

_____

_____

Listening to a Recounting of the Lecture

Listen to the lecture a third time, checking to be sure that your notes are complete. This time the speaker will recount the lecture in a more informal, spontaneous speaking style, paraphrasing and summarizing the information in the lecture.

C. Post-listening Activities

Recapping the Lecture from Your Notes: Presenting the Information Orally

Recount the information you heard in the lecture to a partner, the class, or your teacher. Use your notes to help you relate the main ideas as well as the supporting information that you heard in the lecture.

Discussing Information and Issues Presented in the Lecture

In a group of two to four students, discuss the questions below. Your teacher may ask you to address one of the questions or all of them. During your discussion, use the information in your notes to support your ideas. At the end of the discussion, a representative from the group should summarize the group's discussion for the class.

1. Discuss the roles that the following played in the defeat of the Aztecs by the Spaniards:
   a. superior weaponry
   b. fear of the supernatural
   c. Montezuma's indecisive leadership

   What factors not mentioned in the lecture may have played a role in the defeat of the Aztecs?

2. In Mexico there is a fusion of races, but the country is quite homogenous in terms of religion and language. Is your country homogenous or heterogeneous with respect to:
   a. religion?
   b. race?
   c. language?
   d. social customs?

   Explain each answer by giving examples.

3. Below you will see a list of pairs of people who were mentioned in the lecture. With a partner, plan a role play that illustrates a conversation that might have taken place between these individuals.
   a. Montezuma and Cortes
   b. Montezuma and the messenger who first saw Cortes' ships
   c. Cortes and the leader of an Indian tribe that became Cortes' ally
   d. Cortes and La Malinche

Practice your role play with your partner, and then present the role play to the class.

D. Reading Expansion

Preparation of the Reading Expansion in Progress

Reading a Translation of Ancient Aztec Chronicles

There is a proverb in English that says, "History is written by the victors." That is, the nation whose army wins tells the story from their point of view. The losers rarely get to tell their side of the story. Therefore, most of the histories of Cortes and Montezuma were written by the Spaniards. The translation you are about to read is a translation of a chronicle, or history, written by Aztec writers in the 1500s. The Aztecs wrote down the stories as they would have told them orally. This means the writing has some qualities of spoken language such as repetition. You will read a story called "The Spaniards Arrive in Tenochtitlan" from the Aztecs' point of view.

The Aztecs who wrote these stories wrote their language down phonetically using the Latin alphabet, which was taught to them by the Spaniards. The Aztecs used a slightly different spelling system than the Spaniards, so some of the names of people and places in these stories are spelled differently by the Aztecs. For example, the Aztecs spell the name of their king "Motecuhzoma," and the Spaniards spell his name "Montezuma." The spellings are different, but the person they represent is the same. Don't let the spellings confuse you.

Each section begins with an introduction by the translator. Use this section to help introduce you to the ideas that will be presented in the more oral-sounding translation that follows.

Chapter Eight
The Spaniards Arrive in Tenochtitlan

from
The Broken Spears: The Aztec Account of the Conquest of Mexico, *(pp 62–69)* trans. Leon Miguel Portilla, 1969. Boston: Beacon Press.

Introduction

The Spaniards continued their march toward the Aztec capital, accompanied by all the allies they had brought with them from the Tlaxcala region. The account given in the texts by Sahagun's informants, from which the passages in this chapter are drawn, begins with a description of the order in which the various sections of the army made their appearance. They approached the island city from the south, by way of Ixtapalapa, and arrived in Xoloco (later called San Anton and now part of the Avenue of San Antonio Abad) on November 8, 1519. The precise date is recorded in the *XIII relacion* of Fernando de Alva Ixtilxochitl.

When Cortes and Motecuhzoma finally met at Huitzillan, on the same avenue, they greeted each other in speeches that have been carefully preserved by Sahagun's informants. The texts then describe the stay of the conquistadors in Tenochtitlan and their greed for the gold objects in the treasure houses.

Motecuhzoma Goes Out to Meet Cortes

The Spaniards arrived in Xoloco, near the entrance to Tenochtitlan. That was the end of the march, for they had reached their goal.

Motecuhzoma now arrayed himself in his finery, preparing to go out to meet them. The other great princes also adorned their persons, as did the nobles and their chieftains and knights. They all went out together to meet the strangers.

They brought trays heaped with the finest flowers—the flower that resembles a shield; the flower shaped like a heart; in the center, the flower with the sweetest aroma; and the fragrant yellow flower, the most precious of all. They also brought garlands of flowers, and ornaments for the breast, and necklaces of gold, necklaces hung with rich stones, necklaces fashioned in the petatillo style.

Thus Motecuhzoma went out to meet them, there in Huitzillan. He presented many gifts to the Captain and his commanders, those who had come to make war. He showered gifts upon them and hung flowers around their necks; he gave them necklaces of flowers and bands of flowers to adorn their breasts; he set garlands of flowers upon their heads. Then he hung the gold necklaces around their necks and gave them presents of every sort as gifts of welcome.

Speeches of Motecuhzoma and Cortes

When Motecuhzoma had given necklaces to each one, Cortes asked him: "Are you Motecuhzoma? Are you the king? Is it true that you are the king Motecuhzoma?"

And the king said: "Yes, I am Motecuhzoma." Then he stood up to welcome Cortes; he came forward, bowed his head low and addressed him in these words: "Our lord, you are weary. The journey has tired you, but now you have arrived on the earth. You have come to your city, Mexico. You have come here to sit on your throne, to sit under its canopy.

"The kings who have gone before, your representatives, guarded it and preserved it for your coming. The kings Itzcoatl, Motecuhzoma the Elder, Axayacatl, Tizoc and Ahuitzol ruled for you in the City of Mexico. The people were protected by their swords and sheltered by their shields.

"Do the kings know the destiny of those they left behind, their posterity? If only they are watching! If only they can see what I see!

"No, it is not a dream. I am not walking in my sleep. I am not seeing you in my dreams. . . . I have seen you at last! I have met you face to face! I was in agony for five days, for ten days, with my eyes fixed on the Region of Mystery. And now you have come out of the clouds and mists to sit on your throne again.

"This was foretold by the kings who governed your city, and now it has taken place. You have come back to us; you have come down form the sky. Rest now, and take possession of your royal houses. Welcome to your land, my lords!"

When Motecuhzoma had finished, La Malinche translated his address into Spanish so that the Captain could understand it. Cortes replied in his strange and savage tongue, speaking first to La Malinche: "Tell Motecuhzoma that we are his friends. There is nothing to fear. We have wanted to see him for a long time, and now we have seen his face and heard his words. Tell him that we love him well and that our hearts are contented."

Then he said to Motecuhzoma: "We have come to your house in Mexico as friends. There is nothing to fear."

La Malinche translated this speech and the Spaniards grasped Motecuhzoma's hands and patted his back to show their affection for him.

Attitudes of the Spaniards and the Native Lords

The Spaniards examined everything they saw. They dismounted from their horses, and mounted them again, and dismounted again, so as not to miss anything of interest.

The chiefs who accompanied Motecuhzoma were: Cacama, king of Tezcoco; Tetlepanquetzaltzin, king of Tlacopan; Itzcuauhtzin the Tlacochcalcatl, lord of Tlatelolco; and Topantemoc, Motecuhzoma's treasurer in Tlatelolco. These four chiefs were standing in a file.

The other princes were: Atlixcatzin [chief who has taken captives][1]; Tepeoatzin, the Tlacochcalcatl; Quetzalaztatzin, the keeper of the chalk; Totomotzin; Hecateupatiltzin; and Cuappiatzin.

When Motecuhzoma was imprisoned, they all went into hiding. They ran away to hide and treacherously abandoned him!

The Spaniards Take Possession of the City

When the Spaniards entered the Royal House, they placed Motecuhzoma under guard and kept him under their vigilance. They also placed a guard over Itzcuauhtzin, but the other lords were permitted to depart.

Then the Spaniards fired one of their cannons, and this caused great confusion in the city. The people scattered in every direction; they fled without rhyme or reason; they ran off as if they were being pursued. It was as if they had eaten the mushrooms that confuse the mind, or had seen some dreadful apparition. They were all overcome by terror, as if their hearts had fainted. And when night fell, the panic spread through the city and their fears would not let them sleep.

In the morning the Spaniards told Motecuhzoma what they needed in the way of supplies: tortillas, fried chickens, hens' eggs, pure water, firewood and charcoal. Also: large, clean cooking pots, water jars, pitchers, dishes and other pottery. Motecuhzoma ordered that it be sent to them. The chiefs who received this order were angry with the king and no longer revered or respected him. But they furnished the Spaniards with all the provisions they needed—food, beverages and water, and fodder for the horses.

The Spaniards Reveal Their Greed

When the Spaniards were installed in the palace, they asked Motecuhzoma about the city's resources and reserves and about the warriors' ensigns and shields. They questioned him closely and then demanded gold.

Motecuhzoma guided them to it. They surrounded him and crowded close with their weapons. He walked in the center, while they formed a circle around him.

When they arrived at the treasure house called Teucalco, the riches of gold and feathers were brought out to them: ornaments made of quetzal feathers, richly worked shields, disks of gold, the necklaces of the idols, gold nose plugs, gold greaves and bracelets and crowns.

The Spaniards immediately stripped the feathers from the gold shields and ensigns. They gathered all the gold into a great mound and set fire to everything else, regardless of its value. Then they melted down the gold into ingots. As for precious green stones, they took only the best of them; the rest were snatched up by the Tlaxcaltecas. The Spaniards searched through the whole treasure house, questioning and quarreling, and seized every object they thought was beautiful.

The Seizure of Motecuhzoma's Treasures

Next they went to Motecuhzoma's storehouse, in the place called Totocalco [Place of the Palace of the Birds],[2] where his personal treasures were kept. The Spaniards grinned like little beasts and patted each other with delight.

When they entered the hall of treasures, it was as if they had arrived in Paradise. They searched everywhere and coveted everything; they were slaves to their own greed. All of Motecuhzoma's possessions were brought out: fine bracelets, necklaces with large stones, ankle rings with little gold bells, the royal crowns and all the royal finery—everything that belonged to the king and was reserved to him only. They seized these treasures as if they were their own, as if this plunder were merely a stroke of good luck. And when they had taken all the gold, they heaped up everything else in the middle of the patio.

La Malinche called the nobles together. She climbed up to the palace roof and cried: "Mexicanos, come forward! The Spaniards need your help! Bring them food and pure water. They are tired and hungry; they are almost fainting from exhaustion! Why do you not come forward? Are you angry with them?"

The Mexicans were too frightened to approach. They were crushed by terror and would not risk coming forward. They shied away as if the Spaniards were wild beasts, as if the hour were midnight on the blackest night of the year. Yet they did not abandon the Spaniards to hunger and thirst. They brought them whatever they needed, but shook with fear as they did so. They delivered the supplies to the Spaniards with trembling, then turned and hurried away.

[1]Military title given to a warrior who had captured four enemies.
[2]The zoological garden attached to the royal palaces.

Discussing Information and Issues Presented in the Reading

1. How do you interpret the proverb, "History is written by the victors"? How does this proverb apply to our knowledge of the Aztec empire? How does the Aztecs' story of Montezuma and Cortes differ from what you think the Spaniard's version of the conquest of Mexico would be like? Check your predictions in a history book about Montezuma and Cortes that tells the story from the Spanish point of view.

2. For each of the sections in the reading, identify the sentences (1) containing the main idea of the section, and (2) providing the supporting detail:
   a. Motecuhzoma Goes Out to Meet Cortes
   b. Speeches of Motecuhzoma and Cortes
   c. Attitudes of the Spaniards and the Native Lords
   d. The Spaniards Take Possession of the City
   e. The Spaniards Reveal Their Greed
   f. The Seizure of Motecuhzoma's Treasures

3. List statements from the reading about La Malinche, and discuss your interpretation of how you think the Aztecs must have viewed her. Don't forget to use paraphrasing or quotation marks when you take information from the text to support your ideas.

4. In 1992, the 500th anniversary of Columbus's discovery of America was celebrated. During this celebration, many people expressed the opinion that the European conquests in the New World (as the Americas were then called) were negative because many people and whole cultures were destroyed by the Europeans. Based on what you now know about the Aztecs and the Spanish conquest of Mexico, do you think the Spaniards were wrong to do what they did? Why? Was Cortes a "bad" man and Montezuma a "good" man? How do you know? Are modern-day morals better than the morals of Cortes or Montezuma? Why or why not?

Journal Writing

After the listening and reading exercises in each unit of this book, you will have the opportunity to express your own opinions about the information you have read and heard in a journal. In your journal, write and support your own opinion as you answer the questions in the journal writing sections, or as you respond to questions assigned by your teacher.

Respond to this question in your journal.

In the sixteenth century, Spain brought colonial rule to Mexico. Write about foreign influences that your country has experienced. Discuss the following:
   a. the foreign influences in your country in the past
   b. the foreign influences in your country today

CHAPTER 2

THE EGYPTIAN PYRAMIDS
Houses of Eternity

Think about and discuss the meaning of the following quotations:

"The average person does not know what to do with this life, yet wants another one which will last forever."
—Anatole France (1844–1924)
French writer

"I don't want to achieve immortality through my work. . . . I want to achieve it through not dying."
—Woody Allen (1935–   )
American filmmaker

A. Pre-listening Activities

Preview of the Content

The pyramids of ancient Egypt have fascinated and puzzled humanity for centuries. Just how were they built at a time when human beings lacked knowledge of advanced mathematics, when we had no modern machinery or technology, when we had only copper tools to work with? Certain other questions come to mind when trying to understand the incredible mystery of these fantastic monuments: questions such as why would someone—let's say a king—require that 100,000 workers labor for 20 years to construct a tomb to place his dead body in? Was it his attempt to secure immortal life for his soul when his body had stopped functioning? Was it his attempt to hide his possessions from robbers? Was it his fear of being forgotten—of being human rather than superhuman? Or was it his attempt to be equal to an immortal god? To all of these questions, the answer appears to be "yes, indeed."

In the presentation, the lecturer will trace the evolution and the development of the pyramids, and will attempt to show the human and religious significance of these gigantic monuments to mankind's search for immortality.

Think about this

What's the most interesting structure in the world? The Eiffel Tower? The Great Wall of China? A structure in your country? List three reasons why you find this structure interesting and share these reasons with a partner.

B. Input Models and Listening Activities

Orientation Listening

As you listen to the lecture for the first time, use the outline below to help you understand the general content of the lecture and the topics discussed. The outline should help you perceive the overall structure of the lecture and the main ideas presented by the lecturer.

I. The pyramids of Egypt have survived time and weather
II. The pyramids were constructed as burial places for the ancient Egyptian royal family members
   A. The ancient Egyptians believed in life after death
     1. Prepared for their afterlife by building tombs (pyramids) and collecting possessions to put into the tombs
     2. Had their bodies preserved from decay by embalming
     3. Believed that the dead person could take his or her earthly possessions along to the next world
   B. The tombs were built to outsmart grave robbers, but almost all the tombs were broken into and robbed

III. The structure of the pyramids evolved over the centuries
   A. The mastaba was constructed during the First and Second Dynasties (3100–2665 B.C.)
   B. The "step pyramid" (the typical pyramid) was built during the Third Dynasty (2664–2615 B.C.)
     1. Built for King Zoser by the architect Imhotep
     2. Is a pile of mastabas
     3. King Zoser's step pyramid never covered with stone to give it a smooth surface
   C. The pyramids of Giza were built during the Fourth Dynasty (2614–2502 B.C.)
     1. Located near the town of Giza which is outside Cairo
     2. The best preserved of all the pyramids
       a. Khufu's (Cheops's) pyramid is the largest
       b. Khafre's pyramid is smaller
       c. Mankaure's pyramid is the smallest

IV. The construction of pyramids declined after the Fourth Dynasty
   A. Pyramids offered little or no protection for the dead kings and nobles and for their possessions from grave robbers
   B. Thutmose I commanded an underground tomb be built far from the Nile River and Cairo (in the Valley of the Kings)
   C. Most pharaohs followed Thutmose's example

Listening and Notetaking

Now that you've listened to the lecture once, listen to it again and take notes. The lecturer will present a slower-paced version of the lecture and will reiterate information so you will have time to take notes. You will be assisted in your notetaking by a notetaking mentor, who will ask you to check that you wrote down important information.

Listening to a Recounting of the Lecture

Listen to the lecture a third time, checking to be sure that your notes are complete. This time the speaker will recount the lecture in a more informal, spontaneous speaking style, paraphrasing and summarizing the information in the lecture.

C. Post-listening Activities

Recapping the Lecture from Your Notes: Presenting the Information Orally

Recount the information you heard in the lecture to a partner, the class, or your teacher. Use your notes to help you relate the main ideas as well as the supporting information that you heard in the lecture.

Discussing Information and Issues Presented in the Lecture

In a group of two to four students, discuss the questions below. Your teacher may ask you to address one of the questions or all of them. During your discussion, use the information in your notes to support your ideas. At the end of the discussion, a representative from the group should summarize the group's discussion for the class.

1. Explain why King Thutmose I decided not to be buried in a pyramid. What were the problems? Why had the pharaohs before him built the pyramids? What other ways do you think the Egyptian pharaohs could have solved the problems they encountered with their system of burial?

2. The construction of pyramids was an example of the search for everlasting life. In what other ways have people searched for immortality? Why do you think people continue to search for immortality?

3. The lecturer comments that the pyramids are very puzzling monuments and that many questions and mysteries surround the Egyptian pyramids. As a group, make a list of the questions and mysteries that the lecturer mentioned; then add questions that your group has about the pyramids that were not answered in the lecture.

D. Reading Expansion

Reading a Magazine Article

The next passage is an excerpt from an article that appeared in *National Geographic Magazine*. Before you read the passage, answer the questions on page 17.

1. The following passage is about the Egyptian pharaoh Ramses II. Using the information about pharaohs from this lecture, write three statements you expect to be true about Ramses II. Then share ideas with your classmates.

2. If you were going to write an article about the Egyptian pharaoh Ramses II, what would you want to find out? If you were writing an article for the general public, what information do you think would interest people?

3. In this unit's lecture, the speaker mentioned that the pharaohs were mummified. What do you remember about this technique for preserving bodies? If you could learn three more things about mummification, what would you want to find out? Share ideas with a partner.

The Three Pyramids of Giza in the 1870s. *Photo by H. Arnoux.*

Ramses the Great

by Rick Gore

National Geographic Magazine   April 1991

ON MY LAST DAY in Egypt I finally receive permission from the Egyptian Antiquities Organization to see Ramses' mummy. My colleague, Lou Mazzatenta, is also permitted to photograph the pharaoh. At the Egyptian Museum in Cairo, conservation director Nasry Iskander lifts the dark velvet off the mummy case. I behold the face. Browned and chisel sharp. Arms crossed regally across the chest. A long neck, a proud aquiline nose, and wisps of reddish hair, probably colored by his embalmers.

Ramses' mummification and burial rites likely took the traditional 70 days. Embalmers removed internal organs, placing the liver, lungs, stomach, and intestines in sacred jars. His heart was sealed in his body. Egyptians believed that it was the source of intellect as well as feeling and would be required for the final judgment.

Only if a heart was as light as the feather of truth would the god Osiris receive its owner into the afterlife.

Egyptians did not appreciate the brain. The embalmers drew it out through the nose and threw it away.

After they dried the corpse with natron salt, the embalmers washed the body and coated it with preserving resins. Finally they wrapped it in hundreds of yards of linen.

Within 150 years of Ramses' burial his tomb was robbed by thieves and his mummy desecrated. Twice reburied by priests, the body retained some of its secrets. X-ray examination of the body indicated that Ramses suffered badly from arthritis in the hip, which would have forced him to stoop. His teeth were severely worn, and he had dental abscesses and gum disease.

The photography finished, the velvet is replaced over Ramses' mummy—but the face stays with me. Not the face of Shelley's Ozymandias, not that of a god, but the face of a man. Was Ramses bombastic, cruel, ego driven? By our standards, certainly. He left no evidence of the human complexity or the bitterly learned insights that redeem such proudful mythic kings as Oedipus or Shakespeare's King Lear, but he did love deeply and lose. And all those children who died before him—Ramses knew human suffering. Did he really believe he was a god? Who can say? But clearly, he strove to be the king his country expected—providing wealth and security—and succeeded. He also wanted to live forever. More than most, this man got what he wanted.

Discussing Information and Issues Presented in the Reading

1. What surprised or interested you about the mummification process described in this passage? Tell a classmate.

2. With a partner, list the steps in the mummification process in a chart like the one below. Then consider what each step in the process tells you about the beliefs of Egyptians at that time. Add your ideas to the chart. Then compare charts with another pair of students in your class.

Steps	Our Interpretation
placed the liver, lungs, stomach, and intestines in sacred jars	these body parts must have had special significance because they were thrown away

3. How might someone in the future interpret today's burial customs? What do our burial customs say about our beliefs? Write your ideas in your journal. Then read your journal writing aloud to a classmate.

4. The article states that the Egyptians believed that the heart was the "source of intellect as well as feeling." Modern medicine credits the brain with being the source of intellect, and Western tradition considers the heart to be the center of emotions and feelings. In English there are many proverbs that reinforce this understanding, such as, "Use your head," which means think about something critically, and "His heart isn't in it," which is said about someone who does not really care emotionally about the task he must do. What does your culture consider to be the center of human intellect? Where does your culture place the center of feeling and emotion? Is this modern understanding the same as it was many years ago? Relate any proverbs from your language which reinforce this understanding of the origin of intellect and emotion.

5. The author states that Ramses II "strove to be the king his country expected—providing wealth and security—and succeeded." What do you expect from a leader of a country? Are your expectations similar to or different from the expectations listed by the author of the article? What qualities do you think are ideal in the leader of a country? Why?

Research Project

Individually or in a group, research one of the following topics and write a short paper on the topic, or plan and present a group presentation to inform the class about the topic:
   a. The discovery of the tomb of the boy pharaoh, King Tutankhamen
   b. Compare and contrast the mastaba pyramids with the step pyramids
   c. The pyramid of Cheops
   d. The workers who built the pyramids
   e. The religious role the pharaoh played in Egypt
   f. The pyramids of Mayan and Aztec culture in South America
   g. The life of Ramses II or another ancient Egyptian king or queen
   h. Another question that interests you or your group

INFORMATION RECALL TEST

Part One: Short Answer and Information Recall

Answer each question by referring to the notes that you took while listening to the lectures in this unit.

Lecture Number 1: The End of an Empire: Montezuma and Cortes

1. Between what years did the Aztecs build their powerful empire?

2. Name the Aztec capital city.

3. State the popularion of the Aztec capital city.

4. Montezuma believed that Cortes was a bearded, light-skinned god. Name the god.

5. When did Cortes and the other Spaniards enter the Aztec capital?

6. When did *la noche triste* take place?

7. Why did the Aztecs think the Spaniards were half man and half animal?

8. What were the two names used by Cortes's native woman translator?

9. What languages did this woman speak?

10. List three of the four reasons why Cortes was able to defeat the Aztecs.

11. What cultures fused to form the culture of the Republic of Mexico?

Lecture Number 2: The Egyptian Pyramids: Houses of Eternity

1. For how many years did the ancient Egyptian empire last?

2. How many consecutive dynasties ruled ancient Egypt?

3. What was the main purpose of the pyramids?

4. List three kinds of "grave goods" the Egyptians provided for a dead person to take to the next world.

5. Name the first type of pyramid, which resembled a low bench or seat.

6. Which king's pyramid was the first of the step pyramids?

7. Name the architect who built this first step pyramid.

8. Where are the three great pyramids located?

9. What did the Greeks call King Khufu?

10. Approximately how many blocks of limestone were used to build Khufu's pyramid?

11. How high is Menkaure's pyramid?

12. How did Thutmose I change the way Egyptian pharaohs built their tombs?

Part Two: Synthesizing Information in Mini-Essays

Answer each mini-essay question below in a paragraph. Use the notes that you took on the lecture to support your claims.

1. List and explain the factors that enabled Cortes and his small Spanish army to defeat Montezuma and his enormous Aztec empire.

2. Describe the chronological development of the pyramids in ancient Egypt. Begin with the earliest form of the pyramid and explain how the architecture of the pyramids developed. Give examples where appropriate.

3. Discuss the role that religion and belief systems play in history, using examples from the lectures on the Egyptian pyramids and the conquest of Tenochtitlan to support your claims.

4. Choose one of the pyramids discussed in the lecture. Using information recorded in your notes, write a description of this pyramid.

5. Create a time line that illustrates the events of the conquest of Mexico chronologically.

6. Name some of the problems the pharaohs encountered in using pyramids to mark their burial sites. What steps did King Thutmose I take to resolve these problems? What other solutions could he have employed?

7. Comment on the conquest of Mexico by the Spaniards from a modern perspective. What do you think the world's reaction would be were a country to behave in such a way today? Is it possible for modern people to judge Cortes's actions as moral or immoral? Why or why not?

Part Three: Constructing Test Questions

Use the notes you took on the lectures in Unit One to write three test questions about the lecture. After you write the questions, ask a classmate to use his or her notes to answer the questions.

UNIT TWO

Portraits of Political Leaders: Mystique Versus Reality

Think about and discuss the meaning of the following quotations:

"Good government is no substitute for self-government."

—Mahatma Gandhi (1869–1948)
Indian political and spiritual leader

"Too bad all the people who know how to run the country are busy driving taxicabs and cutting hair."

—George Burns (1896–   )
American comedian and actor

JOHN F. KENNEDY
Promise and Tragedy

Think about and discuss the meaning of the following quotation:

"Let us never negotiate out of fear, but let us never fear to negotiate."
—John F. Kennedy (1917–1963), President of the United States, 1961–1963

A. Pre-listening Activities

Preview of the Content

Millions of words have been written about the life and death of the young American president, John Fitzgerald Kennedy. Much of the writing has been emotional, with little regard for the actual facts. In the following lecture, you will hear an attempt at an objective assessment of President Kennedy's virtues and his faults, his strengths and his weaknesses, his idealism and his lack of realism. The lecturer organizes his talk around the following themes: Kennedy the person, Kennedy the international politician, Kennedy the domestic politician, and Kennedy the social reformer.

Think about this

What do you know about John F. Kennedy? Make a list of five or more facts about this famous American, and share your list wtih a partner.

B. Input Models and Listening Activities

Orientation Listening

As you listen to the lecture for the first time, use the outline below to help you understand the general content of the lecture and the topics discussed. The outline should help you perceive the overall structure of the lecture and the main ideas presented by the lecturer.

I. Kennedy's personal life
  A. A place in legend
  B. A surprising person
  C. Did things earlier than most people
    1. Elected to Congress at 29
    2. Elected to the White House at 43
  D. Mishaps and tragedies
    1. War injury and surgery
    2. Death of a newborn son
    3. Assassination at 46

II. Kennedy's decision making
  A. Questions of how he made final decisions about:
    1. Invasion of the Bay of Pigs
    2. 1962 Russian attempt to install missiles in Cuba
    3. Deeper involvement of the U.S. in Vietnam
    4. 1963 Atomic Test Ban Treaty
  B. Idealism versus realism
    1. Vision of a strong, interdependent NATO (North American Treaty Organization)
    2. The Alliance for Progress

III. Kennedy the international diplomat versus Kennedy the domestic politician
  A. Effectiveness in the world of international diplomacy
  B. Successes in domestic programs—Congressional approval of:
    1. Creation of the Peace Corps
    2. Raising of the minimum wage
    3. Increase of social benefits
    4. Support for space flights
  C. Failures in domestic programs—Congressional disapproval of:
    1. Free medical care for people over 65
    2. Creation of a department of urban affairs for America's cities
    3. Federal aid to education
    4. Tax reform and tax reduction

IV. Responsibility for legislation benefiting African Americans
  A. Bill to prohibit racial discrimination
  B. Bill to outlaw school segregation

V. Social reform in U.S. resulting from assassination

Listening and Notetaking

Now that you've listened to the lecture once, listen to it again and take notes. The lecturer will present a slower-paced version of the lecture and will reiterate information so you will have time to take notes. You will be assisted in your notetaking by a notetaking mentor, who will ask you to check that you wrote down important information.

_____

_____

_____

_____

_____

_____

_____

_____

_____

_____

_____

_____

_____

_____

_____

_____

_____

_____

_____

_____

_____

_____

_____

Listening to a Recounting of the Lecture

Listen to the lecture a third time, checking to be sure that your notes are complete. This time the speaker will recount the lecture in a more informal, spontaneous speaking style, paraphrasing and summarizing the information in the lecture.

C. Post-listening Activities

Recapping the Lecture from Your Notes: Presenting the Information Orally

Recount the information you heard in the lecture to a partner, the class, or your teacher. Use your notes to help you relate the main ideas as well as the supporting information that you heard in the lecture.

Discussing Information and Issues Presented in the Lecture

In a group of two to four students, discuss the questions below. Your teacher may ask you to address one of the questions or all of them. During your discussion, use the information in your notes to support your ideas. At the end of the discussion, a representative from the group should summarize the group's discussion for the class.

1. Has your country had a famous figure who was assassinated or who took his or her own life? How did people in your country react to the death? Describe this person or another famous person from your country to the class.

2. Based on what you heard in the lecture, how do you think John F. Kennedy might be remembered differently if he had lived to complete his term as president? Use evidence from your notes to support your claims.

3. "Kennedy was killed by a lone assassin named Lee Harvey Oswald." State whether you agree or disagree with this statement. Back up your discussion by giving alternate theories of the assassination.

D. Reading Expansion

Reading a Magazine Article

In 1994, almost 31 years after President John F. Kennedy was assassinated, his wife, Jacqueline Kennedy Onassis died. The excerpt of a magazine article that follows is a eulogy, which is a speech or article remembering someone who has died. This eulogy remembers Jackie Kennedy for two things: 1) the elegant image she presented to America, and 2) the way her example helped the nation to grieve for President Kennedy when he was assassinated. Read the article and then answer the questions that follow.

The Kennedys with DeGaulle in 1962.

America's First Lady

by Peggy Noonan

TIME MAGAZINE   May 30, 1994

SHE WAS A LAST LINK TO A CERTAIN kind of past, and that is part, but only part, of why we mourn so. Jackie Kennedy *symbolized*—she was a connection to a time, to an old America that was more dignified, more private, an America in which standards were higher and clearer and elegance meant something, a time when elegance was a kind of statement, a way of dressing up the world, and so a generous act. She had manners, the kind that remind us that manners spring from a certain moral view—that you do tribute to the world and the people in it by being kind and showing respect, by sending the note and the flowers, by being loyal, and cheering a friend. She was a living reminder in the age of Oprah that personal dignity is always, still, an option, a choice that is open to you. She was, really, the last aristocrat. Few people get to symbolize a world, but she did, and that world is receding, and we know it and mourn that too.

Those that knew her or watched her from afar groped for the words that could explain their feeling of loss. A friend of hers said, with a soft, sad voice, that what we're losing is what we long for: the old idea of being cultivated. "She had this complex, colorful mind, she loved a turn of phrase. She didn't grow up in front of the TV set, but reading the classics and thinking about them and having thoughts about history. Oh," he said, "we're losing her kind."

I echoed the sentiment to another of her friends, who cut me off. "She wasn't a kind, she was sui generis." And so she was.

America continues in its generational shift; the great ones of the '50s and 60s, big people of a big era, are going, and too often these days we're saying goodbye. But Jackie Kennedy's death is different. No ambivalence clouds her departure, and that leaves us feeling lonely. America this week is a lonelier place.

She was too young, deserved more time, and the fact that she didn't get it seems like a new level of unfairness. She never saw her husband grow old, and now she won't see her grandchildren grow up.

But just writing those words makes me want to break out of sadness and reach back in time and speak '60s-speak, or at least how the '60s spoke before they turned dark. So I guess I mean I want to speak Kennedyese. I want to say, *Aw listen, kid, don't be glum. What a life she had.*

She herself said something like this to a friend, in a conversation just months ago, when she first knew she was sick. She told him she was optimistic and hoped to live 20 more years. "But even if I have only five years, so what, I've had a great run."

They said it was a life of glamour, but it was really a life of splendor. I want to say, *Listen, kid, buck up, don't be blue—the thing about this woman and her life is that she was a patriot, who all by herself one terrible weekend lifted and braced the heart of a nation.*

That weekend in November '63, the weekend of the muffled drums, was the worst time for America in the last half of this century. We forget now the shame we felt as a nation at what had happened in Dallas. A President had been murdered, quite savagely, quite brutally, and the whole appalled world was looking and judging. And she redeemed it. She took away the shame by how she acted. She was young, only 34, and only a few days before she'd been covered in her husband's blood—but she came home to Washington and walked down those broad avenues dressed in black, her pale face cleansed and washed clean by trauma. She walked head up, back straight and proud, in a flowing black veil. There was the moment in the Capitol Rotunda, when she knelt with her daughter Caroline. It was the last moment of public farewell, and to say it she bent and kissed the flag that draped the coffin that contained her husband—and a whole nation, a whole world, was made silent at the sight of patriotism made tender. Her Irish husband had admired class. That weekend she showed it in abundance. What a parting gift.

A nation watched, and would never forget. The world watched, and found its final judgment summed up by a young woman, a British journalist who had come to witness the funeral, and filed home: "Jacqueline Kennedy has today given her country the one thing it has always lacked, and that is majesty."

To have done that for her country—to have lived through that weekend and done what she did from that Friday to that Monday—to have shown the world that the killing of the President was not America, the loving dignity of our saying goodbye was America—to have done that was an act of supreme patriotism.

Discussing Information and Issues Presented in the Reading

1. The author portrays Jackie Kennedy by describing what she symbolized to many Americans, what some of her friends had to say about her, and how she reacted publicly when her husband, the president, was assassinated. Based on what you know from the article describe what kind of woman Jacqueline Kennedy was.

2. Why did America feel ashamed when John F. Kennedy was assassinated? How did Jackie Kennedy help the people of the United States lose that sense of shame?

3. Why does the author label Jackie Kennedy's behavior at her husband's funeral "an act of supreme patriotism"? Do you agree that it was?

4. Throughout the article, the author hints at ways that America has changed since the death of John F. Kennedy. Read the article again, and describe some of these changes.

5. This article indicates that the whole United States mourned together for President Kennedy and that Jackie Kennedy made this time easier for the American people. Relate an incident of extreme happiness or sadness that the people of your country experienced collectively.

Journal Writing

Respond to this question in your journal.

One of Kennedy's most famous statements was, "Ask not what your country can do for you. Ask what you can do for your country." How does this statement apply to you in relation to your country? What can you do for your country now? What do you hope to do for it in the future?

CHAPTER 4

INDIRA GANDHI
A Sad Song of India

Think about and discuss the meaning of the following quotations:

"The young people of India must realize that they will get from their country tomorrow what they give her today."

"Destiny is something men select; women achieve it only by default or stupendous suffering."
—Indira Gandhi (1917–1984), Prime Minister of India, 1966–1977 and 1980–1984

A. Pre-listening Activities

Preview of the Content

Indira Gandhi of India, Golda Meir of Israel, Margaret Thatcher of the United Kingdom and Benazir Bhutto of Pakistan. These are among some of the twentieth-century women who have been chosen to head their governments and who made and continue to make history. This lecture highlights Indira Gandhi, 1917–1984, whose life was cut short by the gunshots of two assassins. You will also get an overview of Indira's phenomenal rise to power. One of her biographers, Inder Malhotra, notes that, in her day, Indira Gandhi was often described as the world's most powerful woman. This rapid rise was followed by her devastating fall and then by a rapid and remarkable political resurrection a few years before her death. You will also hear some of the compelling parallels between the Kennedy and Gandhi families, selected details of Indira Gandhi's final days, and the enormous effect her personality had on her style of governing India, one of the most complex of countries.

Think about this

Choose one woman you have known personally who is or was in a position of power or authority (for example: a school principal, a politician, your boss). Write about this person for ten minutes and then share your writing with a partner.

B. Input Models and Listening Activities

Orientation Listening

As you listen to the lecture for the first time, use the outline below to help you understand the general content of the lecture and the topics discussed. The outline should help you perceive the overall structure of the lecture and the main ideas presented by the lecturer.

I. A Kennedy parallel
   A. John and Robert; Indira and Rajiv
   B. No concern for personal safety

II. Indira Gandhi's lineage
   A. No relation to Mahatma Gandhi
   B. Daughter of Nehru
   C. Surviving in a political family

III. Early life and marriage
   A. Marriage to Feroze Gandhi in 1942
   B. Birth of two sons
   C. Death of firstborn
   D. More Kennedy parallels

IV. Political life
   A. Adviser to her father
   B. First election to parliament
   C. Charges of illegal practices
   D. Re-emergence in 1980

V. Her assassination
   A. Causes of the attack
   B. Sikh minorities
   C. Occupation of the Golden Temple
   D. Violence against the Sikhs

VI. Final chapter—assassination
   A. Medical attempts to save life
   B. Death announcement
   C. Succession of Rajiv

Listening and Notetaking

Now that you've listened to the lecture once, listen to it again and take notes. The lecturer will present a slower-paced version of the lecture and will reiterate information so you will have time to take notes. You will be assisted in your notetaking by a notetaking mentor, who will ask you to check that you wrote down important information.

_____

_____

_____

_____

_____

_____

_____

_____

_____

_____

_____

_____

_____

_____

_____

_____

_____

_____

_____

_____

_____

Listening to a Recounting of the Lecture

Listen to the lecture a third time, checking to be sure that your notes are complete. This time the speaker will recount the lecture in a more informal, spontaneous speaking style, paraphrasing and summarizing the information in the lecture.

C. Post-listening Activities

Recapping the Lecture from Your Notes: Presenting the Information Orally

Recount the information you heard in the lecture to a partner, the class, or your teacher. Use your notes to help you relate the main ideas as well as the supporting information that you heard in the lecture.

Discussing Information and Issues Presented in the Lecture

In a group of two to four students, discuss the questions below. Your teacher may ask you to address one of the questions or all of them. During your discussion, use the information in your notes to support your ideas. At the end of the discussion, a representative from the group should summarize the group's discussion for the class.

1. What unfortunate parallels exist between Indira Gandhi's family and John F. Kennedy's family?

2. Choose a historical figure from your country and describe to a group of your classmates how this person is remembered. Give reasons why this person is remembered in positive or negative ways.

3. The lecturer says that Indira Gandhi's murder "was undoubtably the result of great friction between the Sikh religious group and the ruling government." What kind of relationship exists between religion and government in your country? How do you think religion and government are related in the United States? What do you think is the ideal relationship between religion and government?

D. Reading Expansion

Reading a Magazine Article

The article that you are about to read appeared in *US News and World Report* on June 25, 1984, shortly before the assassination of Indira Gandhi. Because it was written before the assassination, the article makes many predictions about Indira Gandhi and her family that did not come true. As you read, be sure not to mistake these predictions for fact. The article gives a brief overview of Indira Gandhi's life and prime ministership. The article also emphasizes some of the contradictions between her ideology and things she professed to believe and her actual actions as ruler of India.

Before you read the article, answer the questions on the following page.

1. Read the title of the article. Based on what you already know about Indira Gandhi, why do you think the writer calls her "India's Autocratic Woman of Iron"? Work with a partner to list three possible reasons and then compare ideas with your classmates.

2. In this article, the writer gives a brief overview of Indira Gandhi's life and rule as prime minister of India. What important events do you expect the writer to include? Share ideas with your classmates.

3. This article mentions two contradictions between Gandhi's beliefs and her actions as ruler of India. As you read the article, note these contradictions in a chart such as the one below. Use a separate piece of paper.

Gandhi's Beliefs	Actions That Contradicted Her Beliefs
nonviolence	
nonalignment	

INDIRA GANDHI
India's Autocratic Woman of Iron

US News & World Report   June 25, 1984

She carries the name Gandhi but she bears no relation by blood, philosophy or temperament to the gentle architect of nonviolence and Indian independence, Mahandas Gandhi.

Prime Minister Indira Gandhi is a woman of iron—strong-willed, aristocratic, autocratic and determined to govern the ungovernable.

She has never shrunk from the hard decisions, being quick to call out the army and quell with force what negotiation and reason fail to solve.

When she quashed rebel Sikhs in Punjab in early June, casualties ran into thousands. Her main concern: Preventing disintegration of a nation of 750 million—the world's second most populous—forcibly welded together from myriad religions and peoples.

For the 37 years since independence, India's fate has rested largely in the hands of one family, father and daughter. The Prime Minister, 66, is the Western-educated daughter of Jawaharlal Nehru, who led India out of colonialism and ruled it for 17 years. Gandhi has done so for 15 of the last 18 years.

Weaned on the milk of politics at her father's table, she was jailed by the British in the independence fight, conquered shy-

ness and poor health and became in 1966 only the second woman prime minister the world had seen. Her husband, Feroze Gandhi, died in 1960.

Telling moment. Those who thought Indira Gandhi might be a charming and easily manipulated ornament in her bright saris were long ago disabused of that notion. During 21 months of emergency rule—a state of near dictatorship she declared in 1975—she filled the jails with the thousands who staged protests after a local court convicted her of corrupt election practices.

Although Gandhi often preaches nonviolence to the rest of the world, she oversaw India's uninvited annexation of the Himalayan kingdom of Sikkim. She fought a war with Pakistan in 1971, which resulted in the truncation of that Moslem nation and led to the birth of Bangladesh. She inherited border disputes with China and Pakistan. She has dealt summarily with the long-simmering rebellion among the Sikhs as well as with communal fighting between Hindus and Moslems and between the native tribespeople and the immigrating Hindus in remote Assam.

She embraces nonalignment yet has tilted India toward Moscow in order to build a powerful, well-equipped army, 1.2 million strong.

Gandhi endured three years in the political wilderness when, in the wake of her unpopular emergency rule, the Congress Party split and she was toppled from power in 1977.

In her private life, Gandhi reads, listens to music, tends to her flowers and plays with her pet dogs.

Progress by inches. During her long rule, the poverty gripping most Indians has eased somewhat as the nation became self-sufficient in food production. Yet the problems seem almost insoluble in a land that is forever racked by floods, drought, famine and pestilence—and groaning under a staggering population growth of 16 million annually.

Gandhi had intended to pass power to her younger son, Sanjay, but his death in an air crash in 1980 dashed those hopes. Before January, she must call parliamentary elections. If she wins a new five-year term, many say it will be her last and that near its end in 1990 she will vacate the Prime Minister's job in favor of her only surviving son, Rajiv.

It then would be up to Rajiv, a 39-year-old former airline pilot only now trying his political wings, to carry the Nehru dynasty into the next century.

Discussing Information and Issues Presented in the Reading

1. Think about the contradictions between Indira Gandhi's beliefs and actions. How do you think she would have justified her actions? In your journal, write an explanation from her point of view.

2. This article states that Gandhi's main concern was "preventing the disintegration of a nation of 750 million." Which of Gandhi's actions as prime minister support this idea?

3. The title of this article emphasizes one aspect of Gandhi's rule of India. With a partner, write another title for this article that emphasizes a different aspect of her rule. Read your title to the class.

4. Consider the following questions as you write in your journal. Would you want to be a political leader in your country? If you would, describe what you would do in your chosen office. If you would not want to be a political leader, explain what makes you feel this way.

5. The article lists areas of governing where Indira Gandhi was rather successful, as well as problems that she was unable to solve. The author even suggests that these problems might be unsolvable. Discuss Gandhi's successes and failures as a political leader and decide if you believe the problems outlined in the article are truly unsolvable.

6. Some of the contradictions between Gandhi's professed political beliefs and her actions as prime minister are pointed out in the article. In a group of three to four students, search the article to locate these contradictions. Do you believe that it is wise or necessary for politicians to have contradictions between what they say and what they do? Why or why not?

7. What was Mrs. Gandhi's main concern as prime minister of India? In what ways do her actions prove that this was her main concern? Use evidence from the article to back up your claims.

Journal Writing

Respond to this question in your journal.

In your opinion, what characteristics should the leader of a country have? Did Indira Gandhi have such characteristics? Does the present leader of your country have such characteristics?

INFORMATION RECALL TEST

Part One: Short Answer and Information Recall

Answer each question by referring to the notes that you took while listening to the lectures in this unit.

Lecture Number 3: John F. Kennedy

1. When was John F. Kennedy murdered?

2. How old was Kennedy when he was elected president and how old was he when he was assassinated?

3. In what year did the Bay of Pigs Invasion occur?

4. What multi-national organization was in poor shape during most of Kennedy's administration?

5. State the name of the program Kennedy advocated for Latin America.

6. What idealistic plan to make American technical skills available to developing countries did Kennedy conceive?

7. Who was Kennedy's successor? (Who became president after Kennedy?)

8. The lecturer lists four of Kennedy's domestic programs that the American Congress passed. Name three of these domestic programs.

9. Define the term "minimum wage."

10. Kennedy was responsible for two bills that affected African Americans. What did these bills prohibit?

11. What is Kennedy's famous saying that the speaker quotes at the end of the lecture? Explain what this saying means to you in terms of your own country.

Lecture Number 4: Indira Ghandi

1. Who were Indira Gandhi's husband and father?

2. Where was Indira Gandhi educated?

3. When was Indira Gandhi elected to the Indian Parliament?

4. What happened to Indira Gandhi in 1975?

5. State the name of the second political party of which Indira Gandhi was a member and which she organized.

6. List two of the three problems the lecturer mentioned that caused unrest when Gandhi took office.

7. Name three types of discrimination that Sikh's suffered while Indira Gandhi was prime minister.

8. How many assassins killed Indira Gandhi?

9. Name Indira Gandhi's successor.

Part Two: Synthesizing Information in Mini-Essays

Answer each mini-essay question below in a paragraph. Use the notes that you took on the lecture to provide support for the claims you make in your mini-essay.

1. Compare and contrast John Kennedy's life and political career with the life and political career of Indira Gandhi.

2. Would you call John Kennedy a successful political leader? Why or why not? Would you call Indira Gandhi a successful political leader? Why or why not?

3. Relate the events in Indira Gandhi's political career to her personality as described in the lecture that you heard and the article that you read.

4. Explain how John F. Kennedy's political decisions are evidence of both his idealism and lack of realism.

5. Comment on how tragedy, such as assassination, can change the way a nation remembers its leaders. Use examples from the lectures on Gandhi and Kennedy to support your opinions.

Part Three: Constructing Test Questions

Use the notes you took on the lectures in Unit Two to write three test questions about the lecture. After you write the questions, ask a classmate to use his or her notes to answer the questions you constructed.

UNIT THREE

Ecology and the Environment: Natural and Human Disasters

Think about and discuss the meaning of the following quotation:

"The power of one person is enormous. One person standing up can change everything."

—Daisaku Ikeda (1928–   )
Japanese author, poet and scholar

CHAPTER 5

THE DUST BOWL
Nature Against Humankind

Think about and discuss the meaning of the following quotation:

"Adversity makes men, and prosperity makes monsters."
—Victor Hugo (1802–1885)
    French poet, dramatist, and novelist

A. Pre-listening Activities

Preview of the Content

From 1929 to approximately 1934, the United States experienced a major economic disaster—the Depression. The Stock Market Crash of 1929 marked the end of post–World War I prosperity for the United States. In 1929, prices of American stocks fell sharply. It is estimated that stock losses for the 1929–1931 period alone totaled $50 billion.

The country's economic situation was made worse by the natural disaster that struck the Great Plains states of Colorado, Kansas, New Mexico, South Dakota, Texas, and Oklahoma. Drought and dust storms destroyed many of the Great Plains farms and brought poverty, hunger, and death to these farmers. An account of this natural disaster is given in the lecture that follows.

The lecturer opens his talk with a description of the unusual and terrible weather that hit the United States in the 1930s. He mentions that the North and East of the country experienced floods and windstorms, while the western states experienced unusual heat and drought. This lack of rainfall and the onset of the dust storms brought suffering to people and devastation to the farmlands of the Great Plains states. He talks about the heavy dust storms, the "black blizzards," that destroyed so many small farms. Two specific examples of the black blizzards are given: the South Dakota blizzard and the Texas dust storm. He describes the resulting destruction these storms brought to the small farmers of the Great Plains section of the country. The lecturer here digresses briefly to give a possible explanation of what caused the "Dust Bowl"—the term that is used to describe the area of the western United States that suffered from severe lack of rain and from dust storms in the 1930s. The speaker says that the catastrophe—the disaster— was brought on primarily by poor farming practices. Farmers allowed their animals to eat all the grass and vegetation in the area and planted crops so often that the land would not produce any more crops. He uses the terms "overgraze" and "overplow" to describe these two poor farming practices. The speaker says that this abuse of the land, together with the drought that hit the Great Plains area, caused such hardship for the Great Plains farmers, who were called "Okies," that they fled from the Dust Bowl area to California where they thought they would find work and happiness. He says that for these poor farmers California was their only hope, their salvation. For some, it was. For so many, California was not!

The talk ends with the lecturer pointing out that the Depression years were awful for many western farmers as well as for eastern city people.

Think about this

Recall at least five facts about a natural or man-made disaster that you know happened, or that you or someone you know personally experienced. Organize these details chronologically and then tell the story of the disaster to a partner.

B. Input Models and Listening Activities

Orientation Listening

As you listen to the lecture for the first time, use the outline below to help you understand the general content of the lecture and the topics discussed. The outline should help you perceive the overall structure of the lecture and the main ideas presented by the lecturer.

I.   The weather versus mankind
     A. Floods and windstorms
     B. Cold and heat

II. Ecological catastrophe for the Great Plains
     A. Unusual amount of rainfall
     B. Destruction of farmland
        1. Overgrazing and overplowing
        2. Drought

III. Drought in the Great Plains in the 1930s
     A. First black blizzard—South Dakota
     B. Second black blizzard—Texas
     C. Oklahoma black blizzard

IV. Destruction of farms
     A. Migration from Dust Bowl to California
     B. Steinbeck, *Grapes of Wrath*

V.   Hardship for all Americans

Listening and Notetaking

Now that you've listened to the lecture once, listen to it again and take notes. The lecturer will present a slower-paced version of the lecture and will reiterate information so you will have time to take notes. You will be assisted in your notetaking by a notetaking mentor, who will ask you to check that you wrote down important information.

_____

_____

_____

_____

_____

_____

_____

_____

_____

_____

_____

_____

_____

_____

_____

_____

_____

_____

_____

_____

_____

_____

Listening to a Recounting of the Lecture

Listen to the lecture a third time, checking to be sure that your notes are complete. This time the speaker will recount the lecture in a more informal, spontaneous speaking style, paraphrasing and summarizing the information in the lecture.

C. Post-listening Activities

Recapping the Lecture from Your Notes: Presenting the Information Orally

Recount the information you heard in the lecture to a partner, the class, or your teacher. Use your notes to help you relate the main ideas as well as the supporting information that you heard in the lecture.

Discussing Information and Issues Presented in the Lecture

In a group of two to four students, discuss the questions below. Your teacher may ask you to address one of the questions or all of them. During your discussion, use the information in your notes to support your ideas. At the end of the discussion, a representative from the group should summarize the group's discussion for the class.

1. The lecture gives one example of how the weather seriously affected the lives of many Americans in the 1930s. How does the weather affect people's lives in less serious ways as well as in more serious ways? Give an example of how the weather has affected your life both negatively and positively. Talk about the different kinds of damage that natural disasters, such as floods, earthquakes, droughts and hurricanes, cause.

2. The drought and dust storms described in this lecture are only two kinds of disasters that affect people's lives. What other kinds of personal and natural disasters can occur? Describe what helps people to survive crises of a natural and personal nature.

3. This lecture on the Dust Bowl highlights some agricultural practices that were very dangerous to the environment. In what other ways do people endanger the environment in their business, social, and personal practices? What can be done to decrease the effects of these damaging practices?

D. Reading Expansion

Reading a Newspaper Article

Read the following newspaper article from *The New York Times*. Harlan Miller wrote this article in 1935. The purpose of the article is to describe the black blizzards and the hardships they caused. To fulfill this purpose, the author uses many descriptive words, and tells the story of the blizzards from the point of view of people from different social roles. Before you begin to read, answer the questions.

1. Think of three things you learned about black blizzards from the lecture on the Dust Bowl. Share ideas with your classmates.

2. If you could interview someone who had lived through the black blizzards of 1935, what questions would you ask? Work with a partner to write a list of questions and then share ideas with the other people in your class.

3. In this article, the writer describes the hardships caused by the black blizzards. As you read the article, underline each hardship mentioned by the writer.

DUST RIDES THE WINDS OUT OF THE WEST

A Picture of Land and People Under the Pall, as Soil Is Stripped From the Parched Earth and Borne Away

By Harlan Miller, Des Moines   *THE NEW YORK TIMES*   March 31, 1935

THERE is no escape, no shelter from the dust during one of these storms. Dust is on the tongue, in the teeth: It irritates the eyes and stings the tender membranes of nostrils and throat. Windows are clamped shut, but the dust sifts through to cover everything with a brown film. Cracks are stuffed with damp rags and papers; still it enters. Wet sheets and blankets are hung over doors and windows, but the dust sifts in. To the millions in the path of the dust billowing three miles high, a thousand miles wide, travelling 2,000 miles, the dark storm is an assault by nature more pervasive than any other, a bombardment which can be seen, felt, tasted and smelled.

The dust invades the surgical wards of hospitals: operations must be postponed. It obscures the light bulbs in schoolrooms: classes must be dismissed. Headlights of automobiles barely penetrate the haze: officials halt traffic. So thick and intense is the storm that for the first time dust brings a railroad train to a halt. Mills must close, for the dust is mingling with the flour. Grocers cover their counters; only their tinned and boxed goods are safe.

Families awaken long after daylight and find darkness still upon them, and lights burn all day long indoors. Long-distance telephone conversations are faint, for the dust particles are charged with static electricity and affect the circuits. Women and children, remaining indoors, receive electric shocks when they touch metal dishpans or door handles, and wrap them with

Dust storm in Oklahoma.

cloth. Nerves are on edge, as housewives bemoan the need of taking in their washing and doing it over again. "You can write your name in the dust on the wallpaper and woodwork," they tell each other over the telephone. The rugs and carpets must be cleaned again, the chairs are filled with grit.

"How can we ever clean them so we can sit on them again in white clothes?" they ask despairingly. They remember with bitterness that last year they were

forced to repeat their spring housecleaning in May, June and July, and resolve to postpone the task this year. But habit is strong, probably they will clean their houses as usual and pray for rain.

Those who go to work in the cities become grimy and dirty in a few minutes. There is no attempt to keep collars clean; girl stenographers are as dusty as their employers. The unfortunate postmen, compelled to walk the streets, wrap damp cloths around their faces and wear goggles.

Discussing Information and Issues Presented in the Reading

1. Look back at the hardships that you underlined in the article. Which one would bother you the most? Why? Tell a classmate.

2. Using details from the article, imagine living through one of the black blizzards. Write a short diary account describing what you do, see, and feel on one particular day during the blizzard.

3. Tell your classmates about a natural disaster that your country has experienced. What were some of the effects of this disaster?

4. In your journal, tell what you like and dislike about the weather in your hometown. In what ways does the weather make daily life easy or difficult? When you have finished writing, get together with a classmate and read your journal writing aloud.

5. After reading this description of the dust storms that people who lived in the Great Plains states endured in the 1930s, describe the emotions and feelings you think these people probably experienced. Describe the ways people can cope with these emotions to help them survive the hard times.

6. Describe a serious economic or natural disaster that your country has experienced. Who told you about it? What did they say? What were some of the economic, social, and emotional effects of this disaster? How could the disaster have been prevented? Explain.

7. With a partner, select two occupations that are described in the article. Plan a role play with your partner in which you talk about the dust storms from the point of view of two people in the occupations you have chosen. For example, plan a role play between a doctor and a grocer where they discuss what has happened to them because of the dust storms. Present your role play to the class or to your teacher.

Journal Writing

Respond to this question in your journal.

In "The Dust Bowl," you learned about the Okies who had to travel to a new area of the country to try and improve their lives. How do you think the Okies felt about making this big change in their lives? Describe a time when you had to move into a new place or situation and how it affected your life in positive and negative ways.

CHAPTER 6

THE GREAT FLOOD OF 1993

Mother Nature on the Rampage

Think about and discuss the meaning of the following quotation:

Great floods have flowed from simple sources.
—William Shakespeare (1564–1616)
   English dramatist and poet

A. Pre-listening Activities

Preview of the Content

The Mississippi River is the most important river in the United States for many reasons. In the 1800s, this river, the longest in the U.S., provided transportation for the people in the Midwestern States that lie along the river's banks. It also provided transportation for the products and goods that were produced in these states. It is easy to see how this river helped industry and the economy grow in this region.

In recent times, the Mississippi has not been as important for transportation, but it now provides water-powered electricity for the cities and industries that have grown along its banks. The Mississippi region also has very fertile soil, which means that the soil is very good for farming. Many farmers have settled in this area of the country to take advantage of this benefit of the river.

In 1993, however, the people who live along the Mississippi experienced what may become known as the worst flood in U.S. history. In this lecture, you will learn about what happened when the river flooded in 1993, and how the people who suffered from the flood survived and recovered from the flood waters of the Mississippi.

After giving you a brief description of the Great Flood of 1993, the lecturer gives you some background about the river and its names and nicknames. Then you will hear some facts about the Mississippi River itself. Once the lecturer has given an introduction to the river, she follows with a description of the flooding that occurred in the summer of 1993. The lecturer discusses both the events that caused the flooding and some of the effects of the large amounts of water and mud that invaded the towns around the Mississippi.

Throughout the lecture, the speaker compares and contrasts the Great Flood of 1993 with the storms in the Dust Bowl. The lecturer ends by explaining that, because the U.S. government and other agencies acted quickly, people did not have to leave their homes and farms like the Dust Bowl farmers did. However, the lecturer adds, it will be hard for flood victims to forget the power Mother Nature has over their farms, their homes, their lives, and their livelihood.

Think about this

List a number of rivers you know of. What do you associate with each of these rivers? For example: *I was born near the Amazon River in Brazil, so I associate that river with home and family. I also associate it with beauty and commerce. . . .* Share your thoughts with a partner.

B. Input Models and Listening Activities

Orientation Listening

As you listen to the lecture for the first time, use the outline below to help you understand the general content of the lecture and the topics discussed. The outline should help you perceive the overall structure of the lecture and the main ideas presented by the lecturer.

I. The Great Flood of 1993
    A. Caused misery in the Midwest
    B. Occurred sixty years after the Dust Bowl
    C. May have been worst flood in U.S. history
    D. Caused devastation for farmers

II. The Mississippi
    A. The most important river in the U.S.
    B. Forms boundary of 10 of 50 states
    C. Size = 2,348 miles (alone); with Missouri = 3,680 miles long; Nile = 4,000
    D. Vital to economic development—particularly last half of 19th c.
        1. Provides growth for industry
        2. Provides transportation
        3. Provides water-powered electricity
        4. Mark Twain wrote about the Mississippi

III. The Mississippi and the Great Flood of 1993
    A. Large amounts of rain
    B. Towns were flooded
        1. People sometimes had to travel in boats
        2. Homes were evacuated; furnishings were destroyed
        3. Farmers lost their crops for the whole year

IV. Unlike Dust Bowl farmers, Mississippi farmers will survive the disaster. Why? Because:
    A. Some had flood insurance
    B. The government and charities provided 2.5 billion dollars in aid
    C. The Federal Emergency Management Agency

V. Damage caused by the flood
    A. Estimated 8 billion dollars in damage
    B. Cleaning up the mud

VI. People along the Mississippi will not forget the Great Flood of 1993

harms of nature

Listening and Notetaking

Now that you've listened to the lecture once, listen to it again and take notes. The lecturer will present a slower-paced version of the lecture and will reiterate information so you will have time to take notes. You will be assisted in your notetaking by a notetaking mentor, who will ask you to check that you wrote down important information.

_____

_____

_____

_____

_____

_____

_____

_____

_____

_____

_____

_____

_____

_____

_____

_____

_____

_____

_____

_____

_____

_____

Listening to a Recounting of the Lecture

Listen to the lecture a third time, checking to be sure that your notes are complete. This time the speaker will recount the lecture in a more informal, spontaneous speaking style, paraphrasing and summarizing the information in the lecture.

C. Post-listening Activities

Recapping the Lecture from Your Notes: Presenting the Information Orally

Recount the information you heard in the lecture to a partner, the class, or your teacher. Use your notes to help you relate the main ideas as well as the supporting information that you heard in the lecture.

Discussing Information and Issues Presented in the Lecture

In a group of two to four students, discuss the questions below. Your teacher may ask you to address one of the questions or all of them. During your discussion, use the information in your notes to support your ideas. At the end of the discussion, a representative from the group should summarize the group's discussion for the class.

1. Compare and contrast the events and the effects of the dust storms and the Mississippi floods. Talk about what happened, how long the events lasted, and what kind of damage resulted from each disaster. Then consider how people, their lifestyles, and their belongings were affected in each case.

2. How do people predict, prevent, and reduce the damage from natural disasters, such as hurricanes, earthquakes, floods, and other disasters? What techniques might people develop in the future to improve the ways we deal with disasters? Do you think we will ever be able to eliminate the effects of natural disasters or reduce them so that they do not really interfere with the lives of people? Support your opinion.

3. The U.S. government and charity organizations provided a great deal of help to people who were affected by the Great Flood. Make a list of the kinds of help people received. Do you think it is the responsibility of government to help pay for recovery from natural disasters? How much, if any, of the damage should be covered by the government and tax money?

D. Reading Expansion

Reading a Magazine Article

The article that follows was published in *Time Magazine* in July of 1993 while the Mississippi was still flooding. The article focuses on the health problems that can be caused by flooding. It discusses some diseases which concerned the officials and the causes of those diseases. In addition, the article emphasizes the importance of providing people with clean water and food. It also mentions that chemicals and pesticides posed some threat to people. It is important to remember that the article does not say that these things occurred; it simply relates possible problems. As you read the article, you will notice that the author uses very descriptive language and images to help you build a mental picture of what the area around the Mississippi was like after the floods. Before you read the article, answer the questions below.

1. Think back to the lecture on the flooding of the Mississippi River. What problems did the flood cause? Share ideas with your classmates.

2. Read the title of the article below. What do you expect this article to focus on?

3. Because this article was written at the time of the flood, it can only suggest some of the health problems that might result from the flood. With several classmates, predict what these health problems might be. Then read the article and compare your predictions with the writer's.

AFTER THE DELUGE: HEALTH HAZARDS

By Kevin Fedarko   *TIME MAGAZINE*   July 26, 1993

IF HURRICANES ARE MOTHER NATURE'S BARROOM BRAWLERS, SWIFTLY finishing their business and heading for the door, floods tend to behave more like unwanted houseguests: they park themselves in the living room, tear up the furniture, and generally make a nuisance of themselves for weeks or months before finally having the decency to pack up and hit the road. That's not good news for residents of the Mississippi River Valley, who long after floodwaters have crested will play host to a chocolate-colored inland sea sprawling across the spine of the Midwest—a stagnant, festering stew of industrial waste, agricultural pesticides and raw sewage that laminates buildings in goo and provides a superb growing environment for bacteria. The entire floodplain, says Anita Walker in Des Moines, Iowa, will be a "muddy, stinky, awful mess to clean up."

As the Great Flood of '93 recedes, it is likely to leave in its wake a rash of health problems ranging from disease to chemical pollution. A variety of infections related to sanitation and hygiene, all spread by floodwater, are already giving health officials headaches. Thanks to at least 18 breached sewage plants, microbes have penetrated the nearly 800 miles of piping that keeps the Des Moines area's 250,000 residents supplied with drinking water; it will take a month to disinfect the system. Tetanus is another concern, especially for sandbaggers and rescuers slogging through the slimy silt and sewage-infested waters. And then there is encephalitis, a viral disease that inflames the spinal cord and brain and can produce a combination of low-grade fever, seizures, and even coma. It is transmitted by mosquitoes, whose numbers are expected to explode along the saturated bottomlands in the coming weeks.

NOT A DROP TO DRINK: Des Moines residents fill jugs from water trucked into the city.

So far, there have been no major outbreaks of illness. Health officials say such traditional scourges as cholera and typhoid are unlikely to pose a significant threat, and authorities insist that clean water and uncontaminated food—which so far have been available in most areas—will ensure that a full-scale epidemic doesn't take place. "There's a misperception that every time there is a disaster, people are at risk," says Mitchell Cohen of the Centers for Disease Control and Prevention. "The key elements are providing safe water and safe food. Health authorities know this controls any infectious-disease problem."

Less predictable, however, are the effects of the farm pesticides and industrial chemicals churning in the silt-encrusted swamps and ponds marooned by subsiding rivers. While hydrologists anticipate that the sheer volume of water will dilute and neutralize any toxicity, no one knows what dangers, if any, are posed by toxic runoff from hundreds of submerged factories, fuel-storage facilities and waste dumps. "Think of all this stuff making a witches' brew of new compounds," says Kevin Coyle, president of American Rivers, an environmental group in Washington. "We have no precedent."

There is, however, plenty of precedent for the nightmare that awaits residents when the waters finally recede. Denizens of the river valley who have endured previous temper tantrums of the Mississippi are all too well acquainted with the thick, claylike layers of earth that will coat the inside of houses, barns and machinery, delaying repairs and driving up the cost of recovery. Farmers have an appropriate term for the stuff: they call it gumbo.

Reported by Marc Hequet/St. Paul and David Seideman/New York

Discussing Information and Issues Presented in the Reading

1. The writer of this article makes the Mississippi River seem human by describing it with words that are normally used to describe people. This technique is called personification. Find an example of personification in the article. Why do you think the writer describes the river in this way? What attitude toward the river does the author convey?

2. In a group of three of four students, make a list of the possible health hazards that are mentioned in the article. Next to each hazard, write one or more methods for preventing this problem. List a method that is mentioned in the article (if one is mentioned for this problem) and a method that your group thinks of.

3. With a partner, think of one way that modern technology has helped to reduce the health hazards caused by natural disasters like the flooding of the Mississippi River.

4. What personal qualities help people to cope with natural disasters like the black blizzards of 1935 and the flooding of the Mississippi River in 1993? What would help you cope with such a disaster? Write your ideas in your journal.

5. People in the Mississippi River Valley worked together to help the people in the area recover from the flooding. The article mentions some of the ways people provided assistance including volunteering as sandbaggers or rescuers. What other roles could people have played to help in the recovery process?

6. Tell your group or class about a time when you worked in a group to try to achieve a common goal. What difficulties and benefits did you

encounter during the process of working in this group? It what ways was your goal similar to or different from the goal of the people in the Mississippi River Valley after the flood?

Analyzing an Illustration

This illustration first appeared in *Newsweek* magazine as part of a story about the Great Flood of 1993. The illustration helps to explain a role that man played in the flood by trying to control the Mississippi with levees and reservoirs. Examine the illustration below and then discuss the questions that follow with a partner or your teacher.

NEWSWEEK   July 26, 1993

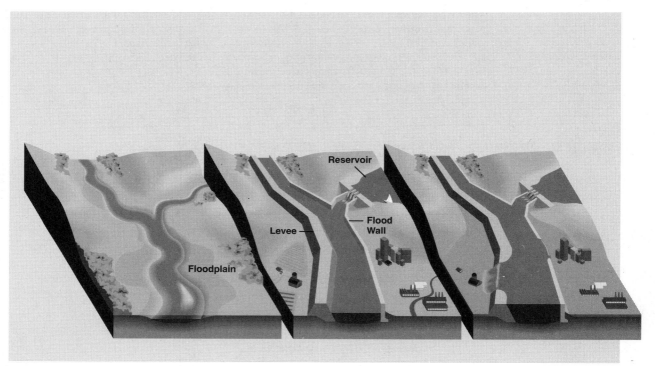

1. There are three drawings in this illustration. What is each one depicting? What helps you to determine what each part depicts?

2. What are the main differences between the first drawing and the second? Why are these different? How do these differences cause the situation in the third section of the illustration? How do you know this?

3. Describe the purpose of a reservoir and a levee. What are their positive effects? What are their negative effects?

4. What is the difference in the flood in the first drawing and the flood in the second drawing? Do you think it is good or bad that these differences now exist? Explain your answer.

5. What is the main point of this illustration? What do the writer and illustrator want you to understand after you have examined the illustration? Are they successful?

Journal Writing

Respond to this question in your journal.

Describe a geographical feature, such as a river, forest, or mountain, that is very important to your country. Describe the benefits that your country receives from having this geographical feature, as well as the disadvantages or problems this feature can cause for your country.

INFORMATION RECALL TEST

Part One: Short Answer and Information Recall

Answer each question by referring to the notes that you took while listening to the lectures in this unit.

Lecture Number 5: The Dust Bowl

1. Which U.S. state had almost 60 days straight of 100-degree Farenheit-heat in 1936?

2. What was the temperature in the state referred to in question 1 on July 24, 1936?

3. What name was given to the strong, hot, dusty windstorms that plagued the Great Plains?

4. What farming practices caused the damage to the vegetation and the topsoil on farms in the Dust Bowl?

5. When did South Dakota experience the first black blizzard?

6. What state suffered the second black blizzard?

7. What percentage of their population did Dust Bowl counties lose to migration during the great period of drought?

8. What name was given to the farmers from Oklahoma who had to leave their farms because of the extreme weather?

9. What is the name of the book written by John Steinbeck that portrayed the misery suffered by the Dust Bowl farmers?

Lecture Number 6: The Great Flood of 1993

1. What is the meaning of the Native American word "Mississippi"?

2. What do people call the Mississippi besides its official name? (The lecturer lists two of these nicknames.)

3. List two ways the Mississippi has helped the United States to develop economically.

4. Name three of the industrial cities located on the banks of the Mississippi that were mentioned by the lecturer.

5. In 1993, how much rain did Papillion, Nebraska, receive in only six minutes?

6. Why is it better for farmers who have farms on the banks of the Mississippi when the river floods in the spring instead of in July?

7. What U.S. government agency helped people who experienced the Great Flood of 1993 by providing them with food, drinking water, evacuation centers, and other needs?

8. What is the estimated cost of the damage caused by the Great Flood of 1993?

Part Two: Synthesizing Information in Mini-Essays

Answer each mini-essay question below in a paragraph. Use the notes that you took on the lecture to provide support for the claims you make in your mini-essay.

1. Compare and contrast the effects of the Dust Bowl and the effects of the Great Flood of 1993.

2. Categorize the ways in which the Mississippi is beneficial and the ways in which this river is detrimental to humanity.

3. Agree or disagree with the following statement, and then support your opinion, using evidence from the notes you took on the two lectures: "The U.S. government should not offer financial aid to people who experienced the flood because they chose to live in this high-risk area."

4. Most of the damage caused by the dust storms and the Great Flood was caused by the weather alone. In some ways, however, people made these problems even worse. Identify some of the ways people made these natural disasters more serious, and explain why their actions had such an effect.

5. What responsibility do people have toward the environment? Should they be held responsible for the ways their actions affect the environment? Explain why or why not.

6. Give specific reasons why farmers who experienced the Great Flood of 1993 generally avoided total financial ruin and the need to migrate to a new state, while the farmers from the Dust Bowl in the 1930s often lost their farms and had to migrate to a new state.

Part Three: Constructing Test Questions

Use the notes you took on the lectures in Unit Three to write three test questions about the lecture. After you write the questions, ask a classmate to use his or her notes to answer the questions.

UNIT FOUR

Contemporary Social Issues: Women, Men, and Changing Roles

Think about and discuss the meaning of the following quotation:

"All the world's a stage,

And all the men and women merely players.

They have their exits and their entrances,

And one man in his time plays many parts."

—William Shakespeare (1564–1616)
English dramatist and poet

CHAPTER 7

THE WOMEN'S MOVEMENT
From Liberation to Feminism

Think about and discuss the meaning of the following quotations:

"The world taught women nothing skillful, and then said her work was valueless. It permitted her no opinions, and said she did not know how to think."
—Carrie Chapman Catt (1859–1947)
   American suffragist

"Of all the rights of women, the greatest is to be a mother."
—Lin Yutang (1895–1976)
   Chinese-American writer

A. Pre-listening Activities

Preview of the Content

The Women's Movement has become one of the most talked-about, and one of the most important social movements of the twentieth century in the United States and in many other countries throughout the entire world. It has, for better or worse, altered the course of American politics, education, and employment, and it has even changed the family structure. As a result it has had a tremendous impact on the lives of millions of American men, women, and children. This lecture deals mainly with the impact of the Women's Movement on the political, economic, and social system of the United States. This does not mean that its influence has not been felt in other countries, however. It certainly has been, and in all probability, its impact will be felt in even more countries in the future.

The speaker starts out by explaining the history of the Women's Movement since its beginnings in the 1800s. She covers most of the major social changes that occurred through the 1900s, as well, and then in some detail, she discusses the progress that has been made in the present. The lecturer explains changes in the areas of the workplace, politics, and the home, which have occurred as a result of the Women's Movement, and she uses examples, illustrations, and statistics to back up her claims.

At the end of the lecture, the speaker explains that although many people still consider the Women's Movement to be a necessary element of American society, many people have differing opinions about the form the movement should take. The speaker briefly explains the term "feminism." Acknowledging that it is a difficult term to define, she, nonetheless, makes an attempt to define the term. The speaker concludes the lecture by stating that the terms associated with the Women's Movement are not nearly as important as the changes that the movement has caused in American society.

Think about this

With a partner, describe two or three women you greatly admire and tell why. In what ways are they similar? In what ways are they different? How would you rank the following priorities in order of importance for each of these women: motherhood and family, professional career, business, political success, physical beauty?

B. Input Models and Listening Activities

Orientation Listening

As you listen to the lecture for the first time, use the outline below to help you understand the general content of the lecture and the topics discussed. The outline should help you perceive the overall structure of the lecture and the main ideas presented by the lecturer.

I. The Women's Movement is a century and a half old
   A. Organized movement began in mid-1800s
   B. Women of that time considered nonpersons
      1. Could not inherit property
      2. Could not control their own money
      3. Could not gain custody of their children
      4. Could not vote

II. Changes in the 1900s
   A. After World War I, many countries gave women the right to vote
   B. World War II—women entered the job market
   C. Today, women
      1. Have gained more job opportunities
      2. Hold positions of leadership
      3. Enter male-dominated professions

III. Women-owned businesses
   A. Among the fastest growing segments of U.S. economy
   B. Employ more people domestically than the Fortune 500 worldwide
   C. Challenge women to find balance between work, family, and social life

IV. Women in politics
   A. Number of female state legislators has grown 500 percent since 1969
   B. Countries that have had women presidents and prime ministers

V. The family
   A. Only 10 percent of American families have traditional working father and stay-at-home mother
   B. Child care
      1. Men playing more active role
      2. Business and government helping
      3. More government-sponsored child care needed

VI. The Women's Movement and feminism
   A. Diverse opinions about how to achieve equality for men and women
   B. Feminism
      1. Difficult to define
      2. Definition from *Feminism and the Women's Movement*

VII. The contributions to society by the Women's Movement and feminism
   A. Society is benefiting from these women's contributions
   B. Women have more freedoms, opportunities, headaches

Listening and Notetaking

Now that you've listened to the lecture once, listen to it again and take notes. The lecturer will present a slower-paced version of the lecture and will reiterate information so you will have time to take notes. You will be assisted in your notetaking by a notetaking mentor, who will ask you to check that you wrote down important information.

_____

_____

_____

_____

_____

_____

_____

_____

_____

_____

_____

_____

_____

_____

_____

_____

_____

_____

_____

_____

_____

_____

Listening to a Recounting of the Lecture

Listen to the lecture a third time, checking to be sure that your notes are complete. This time the speaker will recount the lecture in a more informal, spontaneous speaking style, paraphrasing and summarizing the information in the lecture.

Women's Rights March in New York City, 1970.

C. Post-listening Activities

Recapping the Lecture from Your Notes: Presenting the Information Orally

Recount the information you heard in the lecture to a partner, the class, or your teacher. Use your notes to help you relate the main ideas as well as the supporting information that you heard in the lecture.

Discussing Information and Issues Presented in the Lecture

In a group of two to four students, discuss the questions that follow. Your teacher may ask you to address one of the questions or all of them. During your discussion, use the information in your notes to support your ideas. At the end of the discussion, a representative from the group should summarize the group's discussion for the class.

1. Discuss the roles women play in your country in
   a. the home
   b. the economy and the job market
   c. politics
   d. religion
   e. education
   f. other areas

2. Should women who have children (ages newborn to teenagers) work outside the home? Provide at least five reasons why or why not.

3. Are there fields of employment that are particularly suitable for women? What are they? Are there certain fields that are particularly unsuitable for women? What are they? Explain what aspects of these occupations you feel make the jobs suitable or unsuitable for women.

D. Reading Expansion

Reading a Newspaper Article

The lecture introduced you to some of the roles that women play in North American society and explained how these roles are changing. The information in the lecture, however, is rather specific to the United States. The newspaper article on page 74 focuses on the Women's Movement in another country—Japan. Before you read the article, answer the questions below.

1. Read the title of the article. What does the title tell you about the Women's Movement in Japan? What do you think it means to be "a reluctant feminist"? Share ideas with your classmates.

2. According to the title of the article, the Women's Movement in Japan is not moving very fast. Why might this be so? With a partner, list three possible reasons. Then compare ideas with your classmates.

3. If you were going to write a newspaper article about the Women's Movement in Japan, what would you want to find out? Work with several classmates to write a list of questions. Then look for answers to your questions as you read the article.

Reluctant Feminists

Women's Movement In Corporate Japan Isn't Moving Very Fast

Government Pushes Hiring, But Female Professionals, Firms Stay Uncommitted

---

Dorms, Curfews and Uniforms

Yumiko Ono
Staff Reporter
THE WALL STREET JOURNAL

TOKYO—Yuka Hashimoto was hired from college two years ago by Fuji Bank Ltd. and was assured she could rise as high in management as her talents allowed. She was assigned to the bond trading desk.

Now, clad in a bright pink suit, she sometimes finds herself serving tea to office guests. Her male colleagues never do.

Though she privately complains that the task can interfere with her work, the 24-year-old Ms. Hashimoto gasps at any suggestion that she refuse the chore as sexist. "I'm not saying I won't serve tea because I'm a career-track employee," she says.

Like Ms. Hashimoto, many Japanese women are reluctant feminists. They generally accept the sex-biased slights common in Japanese companies. And when asked to choose between career and marriage, professional women more often choose to stay home. The women's movement here is moving nowhere fast.

"In America, women started a movement because they looked at the situation as a problem," says Eiko Shinotsuka, associate professor of home economics at Ochanomizu University, who follows women's labor issues. But in Japan, she says, "many women aren't particularly dissatisfied with the situation they're in."

Poll Results

In a recent survey by Phillip Morris K.K., the Japanese subsidiary of U.S.-based Phillip Morris Cos., 55% of 3,000 Japanese women polled said they weren't being treated equally with men at work, and less than a third of them said they expected women's lives to improve over the next two decades. Yet, only 26% of the women said they felt a need for a strong and organized women's movement. In a similar survey of American women, a much smaller 29% believed they were treated unfairly at work, most were optimistic about the future for women, and 37% said a women's movement was needed.

Japanese companies dramatically increased their hiring of college-educated women in professional jobs after Japan's Diet, or parliament, passed a law barring sex discrimination in the workplace in 1986. The government's aims were to alleviate a growing labor shortage and bolster Japan's image abroad—not to meet demands from Japanese women.

Unlike in the U.S., where women have aggressively fought for equality, women here have hardly raised a whimper. Much to the government's dismay, many professional women are indifferent toward a long-term career.

Early Bow-Outs

Women make up 40% of Japan's work force, including part-timers, but only 1% of them hold managerial positions. And labor specialists estimate that between 25% and 60% of the women who began corporate careers here four years ago have already quit their jobs. According to a 1989 survey by Labor Administration Inc., a government-affiliated research concern, the attrition rate for professional men was just 11% four years after the start of their careers. The same survey found the attrition rate for all female college graduates at Japanese companies, including those traditional clerical jobs, was 45%.

"I intended to stop working when I had my child," says 28-year-old Sayuki Kanda, who left her Tokyo-based textile company last year after working as a public relations officer for five years. Although she enjoyed her responsibility, Ms. Kanda says she can't be persuaded to return to the corporate ladder. "In the end, large companies are a male-oriented society. It's not a place for women to work for life." After having three children, Ms. Kanda plans to do some part-time work.

But many companies realize that with the increasing labor shortage, somehow they'll have to think of a way to attract more women and encourage them to stay. Sumitomo Bank is hiring 250 women out of college this spring, out of 864 new hires, on a "new career track." Asahi Breweries recently hired 110 women out of its 900 new marketers, and has started sending them to sell Asahi products to liquor stores—long considered a man's domain.

Greener Pastures

Not all of the women who abandon corporate careers return to hearth and home. Some join small companies or foreign firms that have an image of being more evenhanded. Others enroll in U.S. graduate schools or start their own businesses.

Those who stay confront a business

world still sharply divided by sex. The middle-aged men who run Japanese companies expect professional women to tackle work just like men, in an unflagging manner described as "bari-bari"—literally, "a crunching sound." And yet they routinely insist on rules for women that they wouldn't dream of imposing on men. (The 1986 law barring sex discrimination established no penalties for violations.) Some require career women in their mid-20s to wear company uniforms, live in company dormitories and observe a 10 p.m. curfew and get their parent's consent before taking assignments abroad.

A few stodgy banks have a "custom" for a woman—professional or clerical—to quit if she marries someone within the company. The reasoning for this, the banks say, is that if a husband is transferred, as is common every few years, it would be too difficult to also transfer the wife.

Sumitomo Banks insists that women in professional jobs initially wear the same navy blue corporate uniform worn by its secretaries, known as "office ladies" or "OLs." It says this makes less blatant the labeling of career and noncareer women, which might upset the OLs.

No one complains. Kazumi Tamai, who was hired for Sumitomo's corporate research department four years ago, says she accepted the uniform because she didn't want customers to ask why she was the only woman wearing regular clothes. "It's not something to raise your voice about," she says. After two years, professional women may wear their own clothes.

Many confess they aren't as committed as their male colleagues to the life of a careerist in a Japanese company, which typically requires late hours, after-work drinking sessions with colleagues and a pledge of allegiance to the company until retirement. By comparison, the image of a housewife, who is free to go shopping, play tennis and perhaps hold a side job or two, is more attractive to many women. "Japanese men are such workaholics," says Ochanomizu's Ms. Shinotsuka. "The women have doubts about having to work like the men."

They also seem to share Japanese society's assumptions that men and women have different roles. Most agree that when a woman marries, taking care of her husband and children should be her priority.

For now, Ms. Tamai is throwing herself into her career. She eats lunch with the men's group and drinks with them after work. She says her dream is to continue the life of a "salaryman."

Discussing Information and Issues Presented in the Reading

1. What statistics does this writer include in the article? What do these statistics tell you about women in the Japanese workforce? Take notes in a chart like the one below. Then compare charts with a classmate.

Statistics From The Article	My Interpretation
Women = 40% of Japanese workforce but only 1% hold managerial positions	Few women in Japan work in management

2. According to the article, many women in Japan are indifferent toward a long-term career. Why might this be so? With a partner, list three possible reasons. Then compare ideas with your classmates.

3. Use a chart like the one below and identify three ways that the situation of women in the workforce differs in Japan and in the United States. In which situation might a woman from your country feel more comfortable? Why?

Women In The Workforce

In Japan	In The United States

4. If you were going to write an article about the Women's Movement in your country, what title would you give it? Read your title to the class and explain why you chose it.

5. The article states that many people in Japanese society believe that "when a woman marries, taking care of her husband and children should be her priority." Do you agree or disagree with this statement? Why? Explore this question as you write in your journal.

Journal Writing

Respond to this question in your journal.

Should men help with the housework and the raising of children? Explain why or why not. Is it acceptable for a husband to take over all duties in the house if his wife has a full-time job that pays a salary sufficient to support the family? Why or why not?

CHAPTER 8

THE MEN'S MOVEMENT

What Does It Mean To Be a Man?

Think about and discuss the meaning of the following quotation:

"Men are men before they are lawyers, or physicians, or merchants, or manufacturers; and if you make them capable and sensible men, they will make themselves capable and sensible lawyers or physicians."
—John Stuart Mill (1806–1873)
   English philosopher and economist

A. Pre-listening Activities

Preview of the Content

In this lecture, you will learn something about the Men's Movement, a relatively new social movement in the United States—and one that some would call a countermovement to the Women's Movement. You will learn something about the societal forces that have catalyzed the movement and the psychological reasons the movement has gained strength among men. The lecturer will also provide a perspective on the varied nature of the movement, the types of men's groups within the movement and the objectives of the men who work together as brothers under the umbrella of the Men's Movement.

Think about this

Compile a list of qualities which you think are essential for a successful male in the United States. Now compile a second list of qualities which you think are essential for a successful male in your home country. Share your lists with a partner.

B. Input Models and Listening Activities

Orientation Listening

As you listen to the lecture for the first time, use the outline below to help you understand the general content of the lecture and the topics discussed. The outline should help you perceive the overall structure of the lecture and the main ideas presented by the lecturer.

I.   Reasons why did the Men's Movement began
     A. Women's Movement caused men and women to rethink their roles
     B. Men's Movement began to help men support each other in this time of change

II. Two views of the Men's Movement
     A. The Men's Movement as a backlash against the Women's Movement (according to author Susan Faludi)
        1. Men's resentment toward women's professional and personal advances
        2. A similar backlash in ancient Rome when women gained freedom
     B. The Men's Movement as a brotherhood of psychological support for men
        1. Example: father's rights in divorce cases
        2. Confusing images of men in contemporary media

III. Origins of the crisis in masculinity
     A. Changes caused by the Industrial Revolution (according to poet Robert Bly)
        1. Kind of work men did changed
        2. Men no longer saw the product of their labor
        3. Men worked away from home and spent less time with their sons
        4. Young men lacked role models
     B. Effect of the Women's Movement on the Men's Movement
        1. Men play more active roles in child care and housework
        2. Men are entering occupations traditionally held by women
        3. Men have female colleagues whose communication and management styles often differ from men's

IV. Forms the movement takes
     A. Male feminists
     B. Men's support groups
     C. Male activists
     D. Mytho-poetic

V.   What do women think of the Men's Movement?
     A. Many feminists do not like the Men's Movement
     B. Wives of men who participate are often pleased

VI. Difficult to define the movement simply
     A. The movement is like a tree with many branches and many roots
     B. Substantial impact on North American men and women

Listening and Notetaking

Now that you've listened to the lecture once, listen to it again and take notes. The lecturer will present a slower-paced version of the lecture and will reiterate information so you will have time to take notes. You will be assisted in your notetaking by a notetaking mentor, who will ask you to check that you wrote down important information.

_____

_____

_____

_____

_____

_____

_____

_____

_____

_____

_____

_____

_____

_____

_____

_____

_____

_____

_____

_____

Listening to a Recounting of the Lecture

Listen to the lecture a third time, checking to be sure that your notes are complete. This time the speaker will recount the lecture in a more informal, spontaneous speaking style, paraphrasing and summarizing the information in the lecture.

C. Post-listening Activities

Recapping the Lecture from Your Notes: Presenting the Information Orally

Recount the information you heard in the lecture to a partner, the class, or your teacher. Use your notes to help you relate the main ideas as well as the supporting information that you heard in the lecture.

Discussing Information and Issues Presented in the Lecture

In a group of two to four students, discuss the questions below. Your teacher may ask you to address one of the questions or all of them. During your discussion, use the information in your notes to support your ideas. At the end of the discussion, a representative from the group should summarize the group's discussion for the class.

1. Compare and contrast the Men's Movement and the Women's Movement in North America. Consider such areas of the movements as:
    a. goals
    b. activities
    c. effects on society
    d. history
    e. any other areas your group can develop

2. What reasons does the lecturer give for the growth of the Men's Movement? List as many reasons as you can, adding any reasons that your group thinks of. List the four groups of the Men's Movement, and decide if these four different groups have different causes, or if all four groups have the same causes.

3. How are men's and women's roles different in your culture? Are there certain tasks that men or women do not usually perform? If so, what are these tasks? How do men's and women's roles in your culture differ from the roles men and women play in the U.S.?

D. Reading Expansion

Reading a Newspaper Article

On Father's Day, an American holiday to honor fathers, the following newspaper article appeared in the State College, Pennsylvania *The Centre Daily Times*. Before you read the article, answer the questions below.

1. Think of a man you admire. Why do you admire this person? List three reasons. Read your list to the class and then ask your classmates if they would admire a woman for the same reasons.

2. The dictionary defines the word *masculine* as "having the qualities suitable for a man." In your opinion, what are these qualities? List your ideas and then compare notes with a classmate.

3. Read the title of the newspaper article on page 82. Based on the title, what do you expect the writer to say about the "crisis of masculinity"? Share you ideas with your classmates.

4. This article takes a look at the changing definition of manhood in North American society. Three events that contributed to this change are listed in the chart below. As you read the article, look for the effects of these events and add them to a chart such as the one below.

Historical Events	Effects Of The Definition Of Manhood
industrialization	
World War I	
influx of immigrants	

A crisis of masculinity?
Don't worry, it's nothing new

By Caryl Rivers, The Washington Post   Sunday, June 19, 1994

Happy Father's Day, Men of America.

Are you the Sensitive Male, the Post-Sensitive Male, the Involved Dad, the Macho Man, the Neo-wimp or the Terminator?

Confused about the crisis of masculinity in contemporary society? Do you fail to recognize yourself in all the images of manhood bandied about, from the shirtless sex symbol in the Diet Coke ad to the angst-ridden family men in re-runs of "Thirty-something" to the cheerless killing machines of the action-adventure flicks?

Do you long for the good old days, when men were men and guys didn't have to worry about who—or what—they were.

It may be some consolation to know this confusion is nothing new. The crisis of masculinity is not a novel historical phenomenon, created by the women's movement or economic downsizing or modern urban life.

In fact, the crisis of masculinity is as American as apple pie. Teddy Roosevelt worried about it. So did Henry James.

One can imagine Natty Bumpo, sitting on a log in his deerskins, wondering whether the Iroquois had the manhood thing right, and if he had to scurry to catch up.

Every historical era, in fact, seems to have been conflicted over the correct definition of manhood—and whatever it was, people were sure men didn't have enough of it.

In the late 19th century, it was the closing of the frontier that was bemoaned as signaling the end of manhood. Historian Frederick Jackson Turner noted that the "dominant fact of American life has been expansion."

People worried that the end of the frontier would mean the end of the ideal of the unfettered American man, able to push west, to cut down trees, to move elsewhere if things didn't work out where he was—to pull up stakes and move again.

Industrialization and the great migration from farm to city were also altering men's relations to their work.

Before the Civil War, Rutgers sociologist Michael Kimmel points out, 88 percent of American males were small farmers or independent artisans or small businessmen. But by 1910, less than one-third of all men were self-employed.

Manhood was vanishing, critics wrote, as men became mere cogs in urban machines, no longer having control over their labor.

Cities represented "civilization, confinement and female efforts to domesticate the world," as one 19th-century critic put it.

Cities came to represent culture, which was equated with femininity to the point that intellectual achievement was seen to be unmasculine (a viewpoint not unfamiliar today).

The Boy Scouts were founded in 1911 in large degree because of a worry about the "feminization" of young boys who spent their days in the female world of school.

It was against this backdrop that Teddy Roosevelt's hypermasculinity—his image of Rough Riders charging up San Juan Hill, of constant, feverish activity—strode onto the world stage. It wasn't secure manhood that the Rough Rider represented, but the anxiety of the time about what men were, or ought to be.

World War I represented another crisis for the male image; Americans were shocked when nearly half the recruits were physically or mentally disqualified for military service. "In these and other ways," writes psychologist Joseph Pleck, an authority on men's issues, "American men in the 19th and early 20th centuries were having trouble meeting male demands."

Political democracy and the influx of immigrants were also reducing the idea of free and independent American manhood. In the cities, the rows of tenements that housed immigrants with their alien tongues and cramped lives were seen as sapping the vitality of traditional manhood.

The result was a cult of anti-modernism in which men looked to the past for male-warrior role models—to medieval knights, Oriental knights and the Deerslayer. Just as today's men flock to "Lethal Weapon" and "The Terminator" for the comfort of certainty in an uncertain time, our ancestors looked backward to a time when men were men . . . .

If the 19th and early 20th centuries weren't such good times for men, how about the 1950s? John Wayne rode tall in the saddle, Father Knew Best and women were safe at home raising the kids. Surely, that must have been a time when men were secure.

Actually, it wasn't.

As Harry Brod, the editor of "The Making of Masculinities," writes, "The nostalgic male eye that looks longingly back to the 1950s . . . forgets that this was a period of pervasive fear among the white middle class that men were being emasculated and turned into robotized organization men in indistinguishable gray flannel suits."

In fact, as one looks backward through history, it becomes clear that the definition of manhood has always been in flux.

At every crossroads, gender roles were renegotiated, the notion of fatherhood changed and both sexes worried about what was happening to men. Perhaps even Adam spent a lot of post-Eden time wondering why he wimped out and ate the apple proffered by Eve.

As author and essayist Catherine Stimpson, dean of graduate school at Rutgers, writes, "In part, the word 'man' is perplexing because each historical period, every society and each group within a society interprets the raw materials of existence in its own way. . . . Like all human constructs, gender systems can change."

Discussing Information and Issues Presented in the Reading

1. What seems to be this writer's main point? Do you think the writer makes a convincing argument? Why or why not?

2. According to the writer, "the definition of manhood has always been in flux." What three examples can you give to support or refute this

statement? List your examples and then compare ideas with your classmates.

3. This article suggests that male-warrior models such as medieval knights and heroes from movies such as *Lethal Weapon* and *The Terminator* become popular when men's roles are being redefined by society. What male-warrior models are popular today? With your classmates, think of examples from movies, television, and books.

4. The article suggests that male-warrior role models such as medieval and Oriental knights, and heroes from movies such as *Lethal Weapon* and *The Terminator*, become popular whenever men's roles are being redefined by society. List other examples of male-warrior role models. Use examples from movies, television, books, and legends, from North American culture or your own culture.

5. Respond to Stimpson's statement, "Like all human constructs, gender systems can change." What human constructs besides gender systems can change? What changes have taken place in your lifetime or in history? Consider the following areas of society:
   a. government
   b. education
   c. international relations
   d. work and employment
   e. family
   f. any other areas you can think of

Reading an Essay from a Book

This short essay is part of a collection of essays called *To Be a Man*. All of the readings in this book are essays written by men and about men. The editor who collected these articles hopes that the book will provide a resource for men and women who want to reflect on men's roles and men's place in modern society. Before you read the essay, answer the questions below.

1. What is male-bashing? Read the first three paragraphs of the essay on page 84 and then get together with several classmates and write a definition of this term. Compare your definition with the definitions of the other groups in your class.

2. What effect might male-bashing have on men? On children? On male-female relationships? Write your ideas in the chart below. Then read the essay and add the writer's ideas to your chart.

Effects Of Male-Bashing	My Ideas	The Writer's Ideas
on men		
on children		
on women		
on male-female relationships		

MALE-BASHING

Frederic Hayward

"MALE-BASHING" IN THOMPSON, K., (ED.) TO BE A MAN: IN SEARCH OF THE DEEP MASCULINE. New York: Jeremy Toucher/Perigree Books 1991.

By far, "Male-Bashing" is the most popular topic in my current talk shows and interviews. Reporters and television crews have come to me from as far away as Denmark, Australia, and Germany to investigate this American phenomenon. What is going on, they ask? Why do women want it? Why do men allow it?

The trend is particularly rampant in advertising. In a survey of 1,000 random advertisements, one hundred percent of the jerks singled out in male-female relationships were male. There were no exceptions. That is, whenever there was a husband-wife or boyfriend-girlfriend interaction, the one who was dumped on was the male.

One hundred percent of the ignorant ones were male. One hundred percent of the incompetent ones were male. One hundred percent of the ones who lost a contest were male. One hundred percent of the ones who smelled bad (mouthwash and detergent commercials) were male. One hundred percent who were put down without retribution were male. (Sometimes, the male would insult the female, but she was always sure to get him back in spades before the commercial ended.) One hundred percent of the objects of rejection were male. One hundred percent of the objects of anger were male. One hundred percent of the objects of violence were male.

In entertainment, the trend is similarly raging. Some television shows are little more than a bunch of anti-male jokes strung together. Deciding to count the phenomenon during one episode of "Golden Girls," I found thirty-one women's insults of men compared to two men's insults of women. Family sitcoms like "The Cosby Show" or "Family Ties" have an unwritten rule that mothers are *never* to be the butt of jokes or made to look foolish.

As to literature, just glance through the recent best-seller lists. There is no anti-female literature that matches the tone of *Smart Women, Foolish Choices, Women Who Love Too Much, Men Who Can't Love, Men Who Hate Women and the Women Who Love Them*. Two authors told me about pressure from their editors to create anti-male titles as a way of increasing sales. The closest thing to a female flaw that one can publicly acknowledge is that women tend to "love too much."

Products also reflect the popularity of hating men. One owner of a greeting card store reported that male-bashing cards are her biggest-selling line. 3M sells a variety of Post-it notes such as, " The more I know about men, the more I like my dog," and "There are only two things wrong with men . . . everything they say and everything they do." A 3M spokesperson added that they have no intention of selling similarly anti-female products. Walk through any T-shirt store and compare the number of anti-female slogans to the number of anti-male slogans. Women might take offense at

sexual innuendos, but there is a qualitative difference between something that is interpreted as insulting and something that is intended to be insulting.

With news coverage and school curricula fanning the flames, it is no surprise that judges and legislators also punish men. Most people seem to buy the common assumption that the man is always wrong. For example, I have had almost identical discussions with several people recently. Each person first told me that divorce laws should be harsher toward men for, they maintained, it is too easy for men to abandon their families.

Statistics would imply, however, that if divorce is too easy on anyone, it is too easy on women. When I informed them that it is women who currently initiate the overwhelming majority of divorces, they revised their logic: Each one of them concluded that men are so bad that women must leave a marriage in order to liberate themselves from these "oppressive men." In other words, no matter who leaves whom, the conclusion will be always that the man is at fault.

The result is that we encourage women not to improve themselves. So-called "self-help" books simply "help" women adjust to an inferior pool of men. When every problem can be blamed on male inadequacy, women lose the motivation to examine critically their own patterns of behavior. As a result, women lose out on one of the most rewarding experiences of human life: genuine self-improvement.

Very few women have ever been aware of what female chauvinism is, let alone made any progress toward overcoming it. Articles telling women that they are communicative, more empathetic, more prepared to be intimate and committed, more liberated, etc., than men, combined with the still common assumption that a man is not eligible unless he is even older, wiser, taller, more successful, and wealthier than a woman, have produced an aura of fear in women. A spate of articles on a mythical "shortage of eligible men" graces current literature.

Unfortunately, sexism teaches us to think of men as one giant organism that has been dominant for thousands of years, and that can handle (or even deserves) a generation or two of abuse. The reality is that men have the same human insecurities as women, and the generation of abuse has already had dire consequences for male mental health. Boys, struggling with maturation and never knowing anything but the current age of abuse, suffer even more. Relationships suffer as well. In male-bashing times, disagreements lead to the man feeling blamed and the woman feeling oppressed.

Since the dawn of history, the male-female relationship has been able to survive evolutionary traumas by remaining a perfectly balanced system. Both men and women had their own sets of privileges and power. Both men and women had positive and negative stereotypes. Feminist activists were the first to recognize that the system was obsolete, but seem to be the last to recognize that the system was, at least, in balance. They disrupted the system, and that was good, they disrupted the balance, and that was dangerous.

The current male-bashing trend appeals to the female consumer, upon whose whims our economy depends. It is comforting for women to think that men are always at fault, while women are always innocent. Interestingly, male-bashing even appeals to the male mentality. Forced to compete with each other, in contrast to the way women are allowed to empathize with each other, men enjoy male-bashing (as long as the bashee is another male). Males have long had negative self-images, and every man has a deep fantasy that he can be better than all the other men . . . the hero who will earn women's love by rescuing them from all the other rotten men.

For society's sake, however, and for the health of future male-female relationships, we better start to curb the excesses of male-bashing. It does not take many angry letters before an advertiser withdraws an offensive commercial or before a businessperson changes an offensive product.

The alternative, allowing male-bashing to continue its momentum, can only lead to a men's movement as angry with women, and far more violent, than the women's movement has been toward men. It is time to speak out. It is time to recognize that male-female dynamics have been far more reciprocal than feminist theory portrays. To those who insist that the female perspective is the only perspective: Your day has come and gone.

Discussing Information and Issues Presented in the Reading

1. Watch television and decide if you think television is guilty of male-bashing. Do commercials seem to make men look foolish? In situation comedies, who is more clever, the men in the show or the women? Report back to the class and discuss what you and your classmates found.

2. The author of "Male-Bashing" argues that there is a difference between what he calls male-bashing and sexual innuendos that many women find offensive. He states, "Women might take offense at sexual innuendos, but there is a qualitative difference between something that is interpreted as insulting and something that is intended to be insulting." Do you agree with the author? Explain your answer.

3. Do you think that the media should try to be less offensive to men or women? Why or why not?

4. Hayward writes, "For society's sake, . . . and for the health of future male-female relationships, we better start to curb the excesses of male-bashing." Do you agree or disagree with the author? If you believe that society should change its attitude toward men, explain what changes you believe should be made. If you believe change is not necessary, explain why.

5. Does male-bashing take place in your country? Explain. Does female-bashing take place in your country? Explain. Do companies in your country use insults in their commercials? If insults are used in your country's commercials, describe one such commercial.

Journal Writing

Respond to this question in your journal.

Do you believe that men can be good and nurturing caregivers for children? Explain why or why not, and give support for your opinion.

INFORMATION RECALL TEST

Part One: Short Answer and Information Recall

Answer each question by referring to the notes that you took while listening to the lectures in this unit.

Lecture Number 7: The Women's Movement

1. How old is the Women's Movement?

2. The lecturer mentioned four ways in which, by law and by custom, women were considered nonpersons in the mid-19th century. Name three of these ways.

3. What right did women gain in the United States immediately following World War I?

4. In what ways did World War II change women's roles?

5. What percentage of professional American firefighters are women?

6. Women-owned businesses employ more people domestically than what group of businesses do world-wide?

7. Name one country mentioned in the lecture that has had a woman president.

8. What is a major obstacle to women's emancipation, according to Barbara Ryan?

9. What is the title of Barbara Ryan's book?

Lecture Number 8: The Men's Movement

1. Name the author of the book *Backlash: The Undeclared War Against American Women*.

2. Name the poet who is considered to be one of the fathers of the Men's Movement.

3. Name the book written by the poet mentioned in the lecture.

4. Which American historical period do some fathers of the Men's Movement blame for the crisis in masculinity that today's American men are experiencing?

5. List two occupations most men had before the Civil War in the United States.

6. How did men's typical occupations change at the beginning of the twentieth century?

7. Which group of men in the Men's Movement believe that men should be initiated into manhood through dance, mythology, poetry and rituals?

8. Barbara Brotman reports that one woman she interviewed is glad her husband has joined the Men's Movement because they now share responsibility for one area of their family's well-being that was previously her responsibility alone. What is this area?

Part Two: Synthesizing Information in Mini-Essays

Answer each mini-essay question below in a paragraph. Use the notes that you took on the lecture to provide support for the claims you make in your mini-essay.

1. Describe the progress women in North America have made in the areas of:
   a. employment
   b. politics
   c. the home

2. Compare and contrast the Women's Movement and the Men's Movement. Use information from the two lectures to support the similarities and differences you identify.

3. Comment on the usefulness and need for the Men's Movement. Use information from your notes to support your opinions.

4. Enumerate three ways gender roles have changed in the past fifty years in North America and explain how these changes have affected North American society.

5. Choose one of the two movements in this lecture (women's or men's) and identify the stated causes of the movement.

6. Describe specific ways that World War II changed the employment situation for North American women.

7. Provide evidence that North American women are beginning to occupy leadership roles in business.

8. List the four different perspectives on the Men's Movement the lecturer identified and give a brief description of each.

9. Define the term "backlash" and explain why some women believe the Men's Movement is simply a backlash against the Women's Movement?

10. How has the family structure in North America changed as a result of the Women's and Men's Movements? Would you anticipate similar changes in other areas of the world (e.g., Asia)? Why or why not?

Part Three: Constructing Test Questions

Use the notes you took on the lectures in Unit Four to write three test questions about each lecture. After you write the questions, ask a classmate to use his or her notes to answer the questions.

UNIT FIVE

Intercultural Communication: The Influence of Language, Culture, and Gender

Think about and discuss the meaning of the following quotation:

"Language is the dress of thought."

—Samuel Johnson (1709–1784)
English writer

CHAPTER 9

CLASSROOM COMMUNICATION

Language and Culture in the Classroom

Think about and discuss the meaning of the following quotations:

"Speech is power; speech is to persuade, to convert, to compel."
—Ralph Waldo Emerson (1803–1882)
    American philosopher and writer

When you have spoken the word, it reigns over you. When it is unspoken, you reign over it.
—Arab proverb

A. Pre-listening Activities

Preview of the Content

In today's world, it is becoming increasingly necessary to communicate with people from cultural backgrounds that are different from one's own. People, therefore, study intercultural communication to understand how culture influences the use of language. Culture shapes the ways that people use language, so naturally, it affects the language of teaching and learning in classrooms. Classroom rituals, student participation, and the respect students owe and show their teachers vary among cultures. Virtually any aspect of classroom communication can be affected by the culture of teachers and students, but the lecturer today will focus on the three areas mentioned above.

The speaker bases this lecture on the article "Intercultural Communication and the Classroom" by Janis Andersen and Robert Powell. The article appeared in *Intercultural Communication,* a book edited by Samovar and Porter.[1] The lecturer begins by defining the term "communication," and continues with an explanation of some of the ways that classroom communication is affected by culture. Throughout the lecture, the speaker presents specific examples of cultural differences in classroom communication to support the ideas related in the lecture.

Think about this

Think of two or three people whom you consider to be good communicators. What do they have in common? How are they different? Why are they good communicators?

[1]Samovar, L. & Porter, R. (1991). *International Communication: A Reader* (6th ed.). Belmont, CA: Wadsworth Publishing Company.

B. Input Models and Listening Activities

Orientation Listening

As you listen to the lecture for the first time, use the outline below to help you understand the general content of the lecture and the topics discussed. The outline should help you perceive the overall structure of the lecture and the main ideas presented by the lecturer.

I. Communication
  A. Definition from Samovar and Porter
    1. Derived from a need to interact with human beings
    2. Verbal and non-verbal messages
  B. Speech communication—the study of how individuals send and interpret messages
  C. Intercultural communication—the study of how socio-cultural background affects communication
  D. Intercultural classroom communication

II. The classroom and culture
  A. A mental picture of a classroom
  B. The effect of classroom communication
    1. Culture—a system of knowledge
    2. Influences participation and the esteem in which teachers are held

III. Classroom rituals
  A. Rituals are systematic procedures used to perform acts or communicate messages
  B. Examples of classroom rituals

IV. Classroom participation
  A. North American students
    1. Talkative in class
    2. Believe that learning is shaped by talk and participation
  B. Asian students
    1. Less talkative in class
    2. Believe that they learn by listening to the teacher
  C. Vietnamese students
    1. Almost no classroom interaction
    2. Teacher controls the classroom
    3. Teacher symbol of learning and culture
  D. German students
    1. Value teacher's professional/personal opinion
    2. Students do not disagree/contradict teacher in class
  E. Israeli students can critizice teachers if they think teacher is wrong/incorrect

V. Learning a language involves knowing not just vocabulary, idioms, and grammar, but the cultural aspects of the language as well

Listening and Notetaking

Now that you've listened to the lecture once, listen to it again and take notes. The lecturer will present a slower-paced version of the lecture and will reiterate information so you will have time to take notes. You will be assisted in your notetaking by a notetaking mentor, who will ask you to check that you wrote down important information.

_____

_____

_____

_____

_____

_____

_____

_____

_____

_____

_____

_____

_____

_____

_____

_____

_____

_____

_____

_____

_____

_____

_____

Listening to a Recounting of the Lecture

Listen to the lecture a third time, checking to be sure that your notes are complete. This time the speaker will recount the lecture in a more informal, spontaneous speaking style, paraphrasing and summarizing the information in the lecture.

C. Post-listening Activities

Recapping the Lecture from Your Notes: Presenting the Information Orally

Recount the information you heard in the lecture to a partner, the class, or your teacher. Use your notes to help you relate the main ideas as well as the supporting information that you heard in the lecture.

Discussing Information and Issues Presented in the Lecture

In a group of two to four students, discuss the questions below. Your teacher may ask you to address one of the questions or all of them. During your discussion, use the information in your notes to support your ideas. At the end of the discussion, a representative from the group should summarize the group's discussion for the class.

1. Choose one or two of the situations below and describe what kind of classroom and teacher-student interactions would best help students learn in each situation:
    a. learning English as a second language (i.e., learning English in the United States, Canada, England, Australia or another English-speaking country)
    b. learning English as a foreign language (i.e., learning English in your country)
    c. learning in high school in your country
    d. learning in graduate school in an English-speaking country or your home country
    e. learning the most advanced knowledge of a topic in a field
    f. learning as a senior citizen (a person over the age of 65)

2. If we were asked to conjure up an image of the ideal teacher, many of us would disagree on the basic characteristics this person would have. Identify the characteristics that you believe the ideal teacher should possess, and explain why these characteristics are so important for good teaching.

3. It is often said that it is fairly easy to get into an American college, but it is difficult to graduate unless you study and work hard. In some other countries it is considered to be very difficult to get into a university but fairly easy to graduate even if you do not study all that hard. What are the advantages and disadvantages of each of these systems of education? Explain how your country's systems of college admission and study are similar to or different from those of the United States.

D. Reading Expansion

Reading a Research Report

The following research report examines the types of communication that take place in mathematics classes at a university in the United States. Before you read the report, answer the questions below.

1. Get together with several classmates. Take turns describing a typical math class at a university in your country. In your description, answer the questions below.

   Does the teacher . . .
   call on students by name?
   spend most of the time lecturing?
   connect the class discussion to the textbook?
   talk while solving a problem on the board?
   encourage students to ask questions?

2. Read the title of the article. The acronym *ITAs* refers to "international graduate teaching assistants." It is not uncommon for ITAs to teach university-level math classes in the United States. What problems or concerns do you think an ITA might have? With a partner, list several ideas. Then compare ideas with your classmates.

3. Based on the title of the report, what would you say is the purpose of the study? Share your ideas with your classmates.

4. Find the three subheadings in the article. What connections can you make between the title of the article and the subheadings? Explore your ideas as you write in your journal.

The Language of Teaching Mathematics: Implications for Training ITAs

Patricia Byrd
Georgia State University
Janet C. Constantinides
University of Wyoming
TESOL Quarterly
Volume 26, #1, Spring
1992, pp 163–167.

▲ National attention has been given to the concern of university mathematicians and other educational leaders about the effects of having basic courses in mathematics taught by so many nonnative speakers of English from non-U.S. cultural/educational backgrounds (National Research Council, 1989). While Rounds (1985, 1987) and Gass, Haynes, Rittenberg, and Wieferich (1989) have concentrated on the teaching of mathematics by successful and/or less-than-successful graduate teaching assistants (TAs) and international graduate teaching assistants (ITAs), the work reported here focuses on the use of language in the teaching of regular university faculty, rather than TAs.

Arrangements were made with the Department of Mathematics at Georgia State University to audiotape classes taught by three native-English-speaking faculty members: an associate professor, an assistant professor, and a part-time instructor teaching college algebra and precalculus mathematics. In the fall quarter, 1987, two class sessions from each course were taped and transcribed (a total of 6 hrs 20 min). In the winter quarter, 1988, one of the authors attended four classes taught by an associate professor and one class taught by a part-time instructor for a total of 12 1/2 hours of observation. Thus a total of five different faculty members were observed teaching lower-level mathematics courses.

USES OF LANGUAGE

The use of language is the central act in college teaching (Eble, 1983; McKeachie, 1978). During the class session, the teacher is not viewed as a manager of tasks done by students, as often occurs in language classes (Byrd and Constantinides, 1988), but primarily as a speaker (and to some extent a listener with limited amounts of reading and writing occurring in support of the speaking and listening). This project confirms Rounds' (1985, 1987) observation that mathematics teachers can be expected to talk almost continuously during the whole class session. Thus, there should be little surprise that students complain about the pronunciation of ITAs: Faulty pronunciation seems to have become a cover term to mean something like "there is some problem with the ability of this teacher to explain the content clearly in spoken English." The problem may have to do with cultural misunderstanding about how spoken English is used to communicate with U.S. undergraduates. However, the complainers are correct in viewing the misuse of spoken English (in the presentation of content and the maintenance of relationships with students) as central to the poor communication that occurs in many university classrooms.

CREATING CONNECTIONS

Rounds (1985, 1987) reports the use of devices to tie the particular work to larger contexts: (a) comments to tie a particular class period to other class periods and (b) comments to tie a particular problem to a class of problems. Additional contextualizing strategies were observed in our project:

1. Connecting one class to another: "Let's see, that's the way it was on Tuesday. Does that hold on Friday? Okay, right. The same formula . . . okay, right."
2. Connecting the class discussion to the textbook: "If you want to go back to Section 7.1, you can look at these ideas relating functions and their inverses in a more general way."
3. Connecting to the answer key (The teacher and a student discuss the way in which the answers are explained in the answer key, an additional text that students have the option of buying. The teacher advises ignoring the answer key and doing things his way because he is giving the form that will be used in a higher level class, Math 122. Thus, two different connections are made at the same time): "Don't look at it then. Don't look at it. This is a kind of a standard form. You'll see this in 122."
4. Connection to higher level courses: "But this kind of thing will be important in calculus. Sometimes we have what are called trigonometric substitutions and you will have to do this kind of thing. Okay, is anyone going to ever take calculus? Uh, maybe most of you, okay. Well, that's good."

5. Connections to lower-level courses: "And I'm not assuming that you had this in 102."
6. Connections to homework (the teacher is justifying certain questions that were included on a test that the students had trouble solving correctly): "So you did homework problems just like that, too."
7. Connections to tests (the connection most avidly sought by students): "But, uh, to make a long story short, we won't have, you know, I won't, that's not on the test."
8. Connections to other aspects of mathematics: "And, uh, from geometry if you have angle equals side, you always get a unique angle."
9. Connections to the outside world: "Otherwise, when you go home, and I know that you go immediately to the library and read these notes, you would see, well, what's the answer to the final problem."
10. Connections of principles to problems and of problems to principles: "But, if you'll remember the principle that we're saying here, you wouldn't have to [do this whole long process] and that would be real important in the following kinds of examples."

The multitude of connections that can be made in a mathematics course are an important resource for the ITA. Rounds (1985, 1987) reports that the higher rated TAs observed in her project talked almost twice as much as the lower rated TAs. Similarly, ITA trainers participating in the University of Wyoming's 1987 Summer Institute on ITA Training observed that their less successful mathematics ITAs limited their classroom talk to a minimal narration of the problem on the board or did not talk at all while solving a problem on the board. In contrast, the successful TAs observed by Rounds (1985, 1987) and by Gass et al. (1989) along with the university faculty observed in our project all surrounded the narration of the problem with a network of additional information. Working from the analysis provided here, ITAs can learn to provide the networks of information highly valued by their students.

RECOGNIZING INDIVIDUAL STUDENTS

In discussions of the human relations skills needed by university teachers, the comment has been made that U.S. students like to have their names known and used by teachers (Bailey, 1982; McKeachie, 1978). A striking feature of the observed classes is the limited use of student names by these regular faculty members—at least during the class sessions. In the six transcribed sessions, only once did a teacher recognize by name a student who wanted to ask a question. In fact, student names occur only three times in the more than six hours of transcribed materials. In all classes that were observed, names were used primarily for the returning of quiz and test papers. Since attendance was not required in the observed and audiotaped courses, none of the teachers took roll—an occasion in other disciplines for instructors to demonstrate their knowledge of and ability to pronounce their students' names. The teacher observed in the winter quarter, 1988, indicated that he could connect some names and faces during the returning of papers, calling out a name and immediately holding the paper in the direction of the student whose name had been called. Verbal interaction was constantly occurring in all the transcribed classes (as well as in the sessions observed later), but it happened without the use of names. Students felt free to interrupt by calling out questions and comments; teachers responded to those questions and recognized the student by looking in the student's direction, by pointing at the student, and/or by nodding in the student's direction. Eye contact and body language seemed more important than use of names as a method for recognizing students during the class.

Thus, rather than teaching math ITAs that they must learn the names of all of their students (a difficult task made more difficult by the need for the ITAs to learn a new naming system), ITA trainers might provide understanding of and practice with the appropriate use of body language and the language used to recognize students ("Yes?" with a nod in the direction of the student, for example). If ITAs are taught to learn the names of their students, then they must learn to use names appropriately: learning to recognize first and last names and learning which names are used by TAs in that institution's culture (Miss Jones, Ms. Jones, Susie, or Jones, for example).

The verbal and cultural characteristics of the communication that occurs during the teaching of mathematics in U.S. universities is only just beginning to be understood. Methods, manner, and language of teaching at all of the levels that could be taught by ITAs need to be analyzed for similarities to lower level teaching as well as peculiarities of the teaching of higher level courses (for example, one would anticipate differences because of having students who have better skills and greater interests in the content).

Rounds (1985, 1987) has raised the issue of generalizability to other disciplines, especially in the hard sciences. Such extensions should remain at this point quite tentative, in part as a result of finding that so many of our early assumptions about teaching (based on teaching styles preferred in ESL) do not hold for the teaching of mathematics. Moreover, mathematicians have, in personal communication with the authors, commented that engineers and computer scientists do not present mathematics in the same ways as do "pure" mathematicians, with the implication that the approaches to content and to the teaching of content vary significantly even within closely related disciplines.

REFERENCES

Bailey, K. M. (1982) Teaching in a second language: The communicative competence of non-native speaking teaching assistants. Unpublished doctoral dissertation. University of California, Los Angeles.

Byrd, P., & Constantinides, J. C. (1988). FTA training programs: Searching for appropriate teaching styles. Journal of English for Specific Purposes, 7, 123-129.

Eble, K. E. (1983). The aims of college teaching. San Francisco: Jossey-Bass.

Gass, S., Haynes, M., Rittenberg, W., & Wieferich, M. A. (1989, March). Good teaching from an ITA: Compensatory strategies. In P. Byrd (Chair), Language and pedagogy in mathematics: Implications for FTA training. Colloquium conducted at the 23rd Annual TESOL Convention, San Antonio, TX.

McKeachie, W. (1978). Teaching tips: A guidebook for the beginning college teacher (7th ed.). Lexington, MA: D. C. Heath.

National Research Council. (1989). Everybody counts: A report to the nation on the future of mathematics education.

Rounds, P. L. (1985). Talking the mathematics through: Disciplinary transaction and socioeducational interaction. Dissertation Abstracts International, 46, 3338A. (University Microfilms No. 86-00, 543)

Rounds, P. L. (1987). Characterizing successful classroom discourse for NNS teaching assistant training. TESOL Quarterly, 21(4), 643-671.

Authors' Address: c/o Byrd, Department of Applied Linguistics and English as a Second Language, University Plaza, Georgia State University, Atlanta, GA 30303-3083.

BRIEF REPORTS AND SUMMARIES TESOL QUARTERLY

Discussing Information and Issues Presented in the Reading

1. List the types of communication that took place in the math classes described in the report. Then go back over your list and circle the types of communication that you would expect to find in a math class in your country. Tell your classmates about any differences you find.

2. Work with several classmates to plan an orientation seminar for ITAs who are going to teach mathematics at a university in the United States. First, list your goals—what you hope the ITAs will learn during this seminar. Then tell what you would do to reach these goals. What activities would you plan to help these ITAs prepare for their teaching assignments? Choose one person to report your group's ideas to the class.

3. Make a list of Do's and Don'ts for a foreigner who is going to teach in your country. Then compare lists with the other people in your class.

4. The article by researchers Byrd and Constantinides indicates that some problems are created by students who come from countries other than

the United States and who teach American undergraduate students. Many of these problems are rooted in language and cultural differences, and many parents of the American students are very angry that their sons and daughters are being educated by teachers who do not speak English as a native language and who do not understand the culture of the American classroom. How would you defend the use of International Teaching Assistants in American classrooms to these parents? How can ITAs be better prepared to fulfill their teaching responsibilities in American universities? And who is responsible for the "perceived problem"?

5. Agree or disagree with the following statement: "It is possible to be a very good teacher in one culture, and, using the same methods, to be a very poor teacher in another culture." Use information from the article and your previous discussions to back up your opinions.

Journal Writing

Respond to this question in your journal.

Describe one or both of the following individuals and explain why you feel the way you do about the person or persons and what you would say to that person if you met her or him today:
  a. your favorite teacher of all time
  b. your least favorite (most disliked) teacher of all time

CHAPTER 10

GENDER AND COMMUNICATION

Male-Female Conversation as Cross-cultural Communication

Think about and discuss the meaning of the following quotations:

"I am always ready to learn, but I do not always like being taught."
—Winston Churchill (1874–1965)

"The teacher is one who makes two ideas grow where only one grew before."
—Elbert Hubbard (1856–1915)
  American writer

A. Pre-listening Activities

Preview of the Content

The last lecture introduced you to the field of intercultural communication and one area of study in this field: classroom communication. This lecture will describe another area of study in this field that many people do not associate with intercultural communication. This is the study of gender and communication. Researchers who study gender and communication have realized that women and men communicate in different ways.

We learn the communication patterns of our gender from the time we are children. Boys and girls learn masculine and feminine communication styles respectively. Children learn these patterns not only from older role models of their own gender, but from other children as well. Even the games children play help to build these communication styles. The lecturer will talk more about how children learn the communication patterns of their gender and about some false stereotypes people have of men's and women's communication patterns. Throughout the lecture, the speaker will refer to research that supports her claims.

Think about this

What differences have you noticed between male and female styles of conversation in your language? In English?

B. Input Models and Listening Activities

Orientation Listening

As you listen to the lecture for the first time, use the outline below to help you understand the general content of the lecture and the topics discussed. The outline should help you perceive the overall structure of the lecture and the main ideas presented by the lecturer.

I. Gender and communication
    A. Gender is learned
        1. Boys learn to be masculine
        2. Girls learn to be feminine
    B. Men and women communicate in different ways

II. Children can learn communication patterns from play
    A. Boys
        1. Play outside in large hierarchical groups
        2. There is a leader—giving orders = higher status
        3. Play games with set rules; tell stories and make jokes
        4. Command attention by giving orders and setting rules
        5. Winners and losers
    B. Girls
        1. Play in small groups or pairs—not large groups
        2. Play at home
        3. Every girl gets a chance to play
        4. No winners or losers
        5. Make suggestions not give orders
    C. Boys and girls both want to get their way, but they try to do so in different ways.
    D. Comparison of boys and girls doing a task as a group (Goodwin)
        1. Boys had a leader
        2. All girls made suggestions
        3. Girls have a leader when they play house, but this structure occurs less often in girls' games

III. Stereotypes about gender and communication
    A. Common stereotype—women talk too much
    B. Research shows that men talk more—particularly in public settings
        1. University faculty meetings (Eakins and Eakins)
            a. Men spoke more often
            b. Men talked longer
        2. Women professors speak less at departmental meetings (Simeone)
    C. Social concept of what is feminine and masculine

IV. Researchers study gender's effect on communication to understand why misunderstandings between men and women occur

Listening and Notetaking

Now that you've listened to the lecture once, listen to it again and take notes. The lecturer will present a slower-paced version of the lecture and will reiterate information so you will have time to take notes. You will be assisted in your notetaking by a notetaking mentor, who will ask you to check that you wrote down important information.

_____

_____

_____

_____

_____

_____

_____

_____

_____

_____

_____

_____

_____

_____

_____

_____

_____

_____

_____

_____

_____

_____

Listening to a Recounting of the Lecture

Listen to the lecture a third time, checking to be sure that your notes are complete. This time the speaker will recount the lecture in a more informal, spontaneous speaking style, paraphrasing and summarizing the information in the lecture.

C. Post-listening Activities

Recapping the Lecture from Your Notes: Presenting the Information Orally

Recount the information you heard in the lecture to a partner, the class, or your teacher. Use your notes to help you relate the main ideas as well as the supporting information that you heard in the lecture.

Discussing Information and Issues Presented in the Lecture

In a group of two to four students, discuss the questions below. Your teacher may ask you to address one of the questions or all of them. During your discussion, use the information in your notes to support your ideas. At the end of the discussion, a representative from the group should summarize the group's discussion for the class.

1. Explain why communication between men and women can be considered cross-cultural communication. What sorts of misunderstandings might men and women encounter because of their different styles of communication?

2. Compare and contrast girls' play and boys' play as described in the lecture. What are the similarities and differences? How do these different play styles affect the way children learn to communicate?

3. Describe some of the differences between men's talk and women's talk that occur in your culture. As you share these differences with the class, tell the class what other people would think of an individual who adopted the communication style of the other gender. In other words, what would people say about a woman who used a masculine communication style and vice versa?

Journal Writing

Respond to this question in your journal.

Interview five Americans to find out if they think American men and women have different ways of expressing themselves, and how these styles of communication differ. Also, ask the interviewee if s/he can share any proverbs about these different styles, like the one you heard in the lecture about foxes' tails and women's tongues. Report your findings in your journal.

Reading a Book Excerpt

The following two passages are from the book *You Just Don't Understand* by Deborah Tannen. Before you read these passages, answer the questions below.

1. What do you know about Deborah Tannen from the lecture in this unit? Look back over your notes and share ideas with the other people in your class.

2. Read the titles of the two passages. What do they mean to you? Share your interpretations with your classmates.

3. Based on what you already know about Deborah Tannen, what do you expect the following passages to be about? Compare ideas with your classmates.

HIS POLITENESS IS HER POWERLESSNESS

Deboran Tannen
from
You Just Don't Understand, 1990,
New York:
Ballantine Books.

There are many different kinds of evidence that women and men are judged differently even if they talk the same way. This tendency makes mischief in discussions of women, men and power. If a linguistic strategy is used by a woman, it is seen as powerless; if it is used by a man, it is seen as powerful. Often, the labeling of "women's language" as "powerless language" reflects the view of women's behavior through the lens of men's.

Because they are not struggling to be one-up, women often find themselves framed as one-down. Any situation is ripe for misinterpretation because status and connections are displayed by the same moves. This ambiguity accounts for much misinterpretation by experts as well as nonexperts, by which women's ways of talking, uttered in a spirit of rapport, are branded powerless. Nowhere is this inherent ambiguity clearer than in a brief comment in a newspaper article in which a couple, both psychologists, were jointly interviewed. The journalist asked them the meaning of "being very polite." The two experts responded simultaneously, giving different answers. The man said, "Subservience." The woman said, "Sensitivity." Both experts were right, but each was describing the view of a different gender.

Experts and nonexperts alike tend to see anything women do as evidence of powerlessness. The same newspaper article quotes another psychologist as saying, "A man might ask a woman, 'Will you please go to the store?' where a woman might say, 'Gee, I really need a few things from the store, but I'm so tired.'" The woman's style is called "covert," a term suggesting negative qualities like being "sneaky" and "underhanded." The reasons offered for this is power: The woman doesn't feel she has a right to ask directly.

Granted, women have lower status than men in our [American] society. But this is not necessarily why they prefer not to make outright demands. The explanation for a woman's indirectness could just as well be her seeking connection. If you get your way as a result of having demanded it, the payoff is satisfying in terms of status: You're one-up because others are doing as you told them. But if you get your way because others happened to want the same thing, or because they offered freely, the payoff is rapport. You're neither one-up nor one-down but happily connected to others whose wants are the same as yours. Furthermore, if indirectness is understood by both parties, then there is nothing covert about it: That a request is being made is clear. Calling an indirect communication covert reflects the view of someone for whom the direct style seems "natural" and "logical"—a view more common among men.

Indirectness itself does not reflect powerlessness. It is easy to think of situations where indirectness is the prerogative of others in power. For example, a wealthy couple who knows that their servants will do their bidding need not give direct orders, but can simply state wishes: The woman of the house says, "It's chilly in here," and the servant sets about raising the temperature. The man of the house says, "It's dinner time," and the servant sees about having dinner served. Perhaps the ultimate indirectness is getting someone to do something without saying anything at all: The hostess rings a bell and the maid brings the next course; or a parent enters the room where children are misbehaving and stands with hands on hips, and the children immediately stop what they're doing.

Entire cultures operate on elaborate systems of indirectness. For example, I discovered in a small research project that most Greeks assumed that a wife who asked, "Would you like to go to the party?" was hinting that she wanted to go. They felt that she wouldn't bring it up if she didn't want to go. Furthermore, they felt, she would not state her preference outright because that would sound like a demand. Indirectness was the appropriate means for communicating her preference.

Japanese culture has developed indirectness to a fine art. For example, a Japanese anthropologist, Harumi Befu, explains the delicate exchange of indirectness required by a simple invitation to lunch. When his friend extended the invitation, Befu first had to determine whether it was meant literally or just *pro forma*, much as an American might say, "We'll have to have you over for dinner some time" but would not expect you to turn up at the door. Having decided the invitation was meant literally and having accepted, Befu was then asked what he would like to eat. Following custom, he said anything would do, but his friend, also following custom, pressed him to specify. Host and guest repeated this exchange an appropriate number of times, until Befu deemed it polite to answer the question—politely—by saying that tea over rice would be fine. When he arrived for lunch, he was indeed served tea over rice—as the last course of a sumptuous meal. Befu was not surprised by the feast, because he knew that protocol required it. Had he been given what he asked for, he would have been insulted. But protocol also required that he make a great show of being surprised.

This account of mutual indirectness in a lunch invitation may strike Americans as excessive. But far more cultures in the world use elaborate systems of indirectness than value directness. Only modern Western societies place a priority on direct communication, and even for us it is more a value than a practice.

Evidence from other cultures also makes it clear that indirectness does not in itself reflect low status. Rather, our assumptions about the status of women compel us to interpret anything they do as reflecting low status. Anthropologist Elinor Keenan, for example, found that in a Malagasy-speaking village on the island of Madagascar, it is women who are direct and men who are indirect. And the villagers see the men's indirect way of speaking, using metaphors and proverbs, as the better way. For them, indirectness, like the men who use it, has high status. They regard women's direct style as clumsy and crude, debasing the beautiful subtlety of men's language. Whether women or men are direct or indirect differs; what remains constant is that the women's style is negatively valuated—seen as lower in status than the men's.

(pp. 224–227)

IT'S DIFFERENT COMING FROM A MAN

Research from our own [American] culture provides many examples of the same behavior being interpreted differently depending on whether it's done by women or men. Take, for example, the case of "tag questions"—statements with little questions added onto the end, as in "It's a nice day, isn't it?" Linguist Robin Lakoff first pointed out that many women use more tag questions than men. Though studies seeking to test Lakoff's observations have had somewhat mixed results, most support it. Jacqueline

Sachs, observing the language of children as young as two to five, found that girls used more than twice as many tag questions as boys. And research has shown that women *expect* women to use tags. Psychologists David and Robert Diegler conducted an experiment asking adults to guess the sex of speakers. Sure enough, the stereotype held: Subjects guessed a woman was speaking when tags were used, a man when they weren't. The stereotype can actually be more compelling than reality: In another experiment, psychologists Nora Newcombe and Diane Anrskoff presented adults with communications in which men and women used equal numbers of tag questions, and found that their subjects thought the women had used more.

Most troubling of all, women and men are judged differently even if they speak the same way. Communications research Patricia Hayes Bradley found that when women used tag questions and disclaimers, subjects judged them as less intelligent and knowledgeable, *but men who advanced arguments without support were not.* In other words, talking the same way does not have this effect on men. So it is not the ways of talking that are having the effect so much as people's attitudes toward women and men.

Many other studies have had similar results. Psychologists John and Sandra Condry asked subjects to interpret why an infant was crying. If they had been told the baby was a boy, subjects thought he was angry, but if they had been told it was a girl, they thought she was afraid. Anne Macke and Laurel Richardson, with Judith Cook, discovered that when students judged professors, generating more class discussion was taken to be a sign of incompetence—only if the professor was female.

(pp. 227–228)

Discussing Information and Issues Presented in the Reading

1. What would you say is Tannen's main point in the first passage? Try to summarize her main point in one sentence. Then compare sentences with your classmates.

2. Think about how a woman from your culture might
   a. apologize for being late.
   b. ask a friend for a favor.
   c. respond when a friend is late.

   Now think how a man might respond in these situations. Based on your answers, would you say that men and women in your culture communicate differently? Share your thoughts with your classmates.

3. Choose one of the situations below to role play with a partner. Practice your conversation and then role play it for your classmates.
   a. a man invites a woman to lunch and she declines
   b. a man invites a male friend to lunch and he declines
   c. a woman needs her husband to help with something at home
   d. a man needs his wife to help with something at home
   e. a student asks a professor for an extra day to complete an assignment that is due

4. What are some politeness strategies that exist in your native language? Are these strategies similar to or different from politeness strategies in English? Describe these differences to the class and relate any miscommunication that you think could occur between people from North America and your culture.

INFORMATION RECALL TEST

Part One: Short Answer and Information Recall

Answer each question by referring to the notes that you took while listening to the lectures in this unit.

Lecture Number 9: Classroom Communication

1. Define the term "communication."

2. What is the title of the article by Andersen and Powell on which this lecture is based?

3. Define ritual and give one example of a classroom ritual.

4. Which group of students mentioned in the lecture generally believe that they will learn best by listening to and absorbing the knowledge being given to them by the teacher?

5. In which country is classroom interaction very tightly controlled by the teacher according to Andersen and Powell?

6. Which culture mentioned considers teachers to be honored members of society?

7. According to the lecture, students of what nationality value the personal opinions of the intructor and do not customarily disagree with a teacher?

Lecture Number 10: Gender and Communication

1. Define *gender*.

2. Who wrote the book *You Just Don't Understand*?

3. List three characteristics of typical boys' play.

4. List three characteristics of typical girls' play.

5. In Marjorie Harnass Goodwin's research, what task did the girls perform?

6. How does the structure of the girls' game "house" differ from the structure of other girls' games like hopscotch and jump rope?

7. What common stereotype about women is disproved by the studies that examined talk by male and female professors in university meetings?

8. Name the culture in which a wife is expected to paraphrase any words that sound like the name of her father-in-law or brothers.

Part Two: Synthesizing Information in Mini-Essays

Answer each mini-essay question below in a paragraph. Use the notes that you took on the lecture to provide support for the claims you make in your mini-essay.

1. Explain how people's perceptions of reality and their behavior are shaped by culture. Consider an individual's mental picture of a classroom and the stereotype that women talk more than men when answering.

2. Analyze the ways that children's play can shape the patterns of communication children later adopt when they grow up.

3. Compare and contrast the communication patterns in typical North American boys' games and typical North American girls' games.

4. Name two aspects of communication that are affected by culture and provide specific examples of how these aspects of communication differ among cultures.

5. Agree or disagree with the following statement: "Male-female conversation is not cross-cultural communication." Be sure to support your argument with facts and details.

6. Define cross-cultural communication using examples from the two lectures.

Part Three: Constructing Test Questions

Use the notes you took on the lectures in Unit Five to write three test questions about the lecture. After you write the questions, ask a classmate to use his or her notes to answer the questions.

APPENDIX:
SCRIPTS
AND
ANSWER KEYS

History: The Passing of Time and Civilizations

ORIENTATION LISTENING SCRIPT

During the fifteenth century—to be more specific, between the years 1423 and 1440—the Aztec Indians built the most powerful empire ever known in Mexico. The Aztecs had subjugated and dominated the entire area that is today Mexico City. At one time, the Aztec Empire extended from Mexico City as far south as Guatemala. The capital city of the empire, Tenochtitlan, contained beautiful buildings, well-stocked marketplaces, and the remarkable pyramid-temples. On the altars of these temples, thousands of human sacrifices to the Aztec gods were made. Some of these human sacrifices, usually Indian prisoners of war, had their hearts literally ripped out of their bodies.

Some 300,000 people lived in the Aztec capital. It was, in fact, one of the largest cities in the sixteenth-century world. It was five times larger than sixteenth-century London. The Aztecs were fierce fighters and the capital city of their empire was indeed a military fortress filled with soldiers. You know, the military intelligence system of the empire was so amazingly effective that their leader Montezuma knew that strange men—the Spaniards—were approaching his capital city long before they were anywhere near it. He also knew exactly how the Spanish soldiers rode horses and how they fired guns. Montezuma, by the way, ruled between the years 1480 and 1520.

And yet, in spite of his early-warning system, an army of only 553 Spanish soldiers managed to conquer the most powerful, advanced militaristic empire of the New World. How, indeed, was this possible? Why did it happen? Let's go back a bit.

In the spring of the year 1519, an Indian runner from the Gulf Coast area of the Aztec Empire gave a strange report to Montezuma. He said that he had seen two floating mountains—they were, of course, Spanish ships— and that out of these floating mountains, strangely dressed men had come— these men were the Spanish soldiers. The Indian said that the men had beards and that their skin was very white. When the emperor heard this report, he nervously remembered the Aztec legend of the bearded, light-skinned god, Quetzalcoatl. According to the legend, this god was supposed to return to earth one day to claim his kingdom, which was, at that time, the Aztec Empire. So, Montezuma mistakenly, but perhaps understandably, assumed that Hernan Cortes, the leader of the soldiers of Spain, was the expected god, Quetzalcoatl. So he offered no resistance whatsoever to the approaching Spaniard and his small army. Instead, he sent presents of gold and silver to the approaching conquistadores. He asked them politely to leave his empire, but when the Spaniards saw the presents of gold and silver, they were even more excited and determined to conquer this empire for Spain and, of course, to steal its gold and silver.

In November of 1519, the Spaniards entered the capital city and took the emperor Montezuma prisoner. It was not until June of 1520 that the Aztecs rebelled against the small army of Spaniards. Montezuma was killed during this rebellion. He was, so the story goes, stoned to death by his own people, but no one really knows whether it was the Spaniards or the Aztecs who caused Montezuma's death. Many Spanish soldiers were killed on what has been named *la noche triste*—"the sorrowful night"—which occurred on June 30, 1520.

Cortes, who had been away from the capital at the start of the uprising, returned and attacked the city. According to Cortes's own figures, on one day of fighting for the capture of the Aztec capital, 40,000 Aztecs died; on another, 12,000 were killed; and on another day of the battle, 6,000 were killed by Spanish guns. The Indians, you see, were fighting with clubs and spears; the Spaniards with guns. The battle went on for 75 days, and finally, on August 31, 1520, the greatest city of the Aztec Empire fell and was completely destroyed. Cortes founded Mexico City on its ruins.

Again, the question arises: How could an expedition of only 553 Spaniards manage to conquer the most powerful, warlike empire of the New World? Well, as I already mentioned, the prophecy of a returning god completely immobilized the leader of the empire. Montezuma didn't know exactly what to do as he awaited the arrival of what he thought was a god. Furthermore, this god was accompanied by an army of gods who could fire flashes of lightning. (Remember, the Aztecs had never seen guns.) To make matters worse, the gods seemed to be half man and half animal. (The Spaniards rode on horses—the Aztecs had also never seen horses before.) To the Indians, the Spaniards must have looked like what men from Mars would look like to us today!

Another important factor in the Aztecs' conquest was Cortes's use of Indian allies. He used Indian against Indian, so to speak. Cortes convinced the various Indian tribes to ally themselves with him against their hated enemies, the Aztecs. So, all along his march from the sea, Cortes gathered Indian allies until his small expedition of 553 Spanish adventurers increased to an army of over 75,000 fighting men. His success in gathering Indian allies was largely due to an Indian woman known as La Malinche. That's spelled L-a M-a-l-i-n-c-h-e. La Malinche, who was also called Doña Marina, spoke the languages of both the Aztec and Mayan Indians. As a result, Cortes, through her, could communicate in the two major Indian languages. So, she was a great help to Cortes in his negotiations with the Indians and even with the Emperor Montezuma himself. In effect, she helped bring about the fall of the Aztec Empire.

And so we can perhaps sum up some of the major factors involved in the conquest of one of the greatest empires ever known. To begin with, I'll cite man's fear of the supernatural—the fear of the appearance of a legendary god; second, let me cite the Spaniards' military superiority in the area of weapons—Spanish guns as opposed to Indian clubs; third, the tool of political intrigue—the turning of Indian against Indian; and last, but certainly not of least importance, the human thirst for adventure and the factor of human greed—the conquistadores were seeking gold and silver, and they did not care in the least if an empire and a culture were completely destroyed to satisfy their greed. All these factors, and some others not even touched upon here, led to the downfall of the mighty Aztec Empire. And yet, after its fall, another nation emerged, one which turned out to be a fusion of Indian and European culture. This cultural fusion eventually led to the overthrow of colonial rule and to the establishment of the Republic of Mexico.

LISTENING AND NOTETAKING SCRIPT

During the fifteenth century, the Aztec Indians built the most powerful empire ever known in Mexico. Let me be a little more specific. Between the years 1423 and 1440, the Aztecs build their powerful empire. The Aztecs had subjugated and dominated the entire area that is today Mexico City. In fact, at one time, the Aztec Empire extended from Mexico City as far south as Guatemala. The capital city of the Aztec empire was called Tenochtitlan. I'll spell that name for you. It's T-e-n-o-c-h-t-i-t-l-a-n. Tenochtitlan contained beautiful buildings, well-stocked marketplaces, and the remarkable pyramid-temples. On the altars of these pyramid-temples, thousands of human sacrifices to the Aztec gods were made. Who did they sacrifice? Well, some of these human sacrifices were Indian prisoners of war, and these prisoners had their hearts literally ripped out of their bodies.

Let me review for you some of the information you just heard to help you with your notetaking. Check your notes and fill in any information you didn't have time to take down the first time you heard it. If you didn't get a chance to write down all that you wanted to write down, did you at least make some notations so that you could review the notes later and complete the missing information? Well, let's see. The lecturer began the lecture by giving the general time frame of the Aztec Empire and then giving some specific dates. He said "During the fifteenth century, the Aztec Indians built the most powerful empire even known in Mexico. What were those specific dates? (Pause.) They were 1423 to 1440. Where did the speaker say the empire extended from and to? Did you have time to accurately spell the capital city of the empire, Tenochtitlan? Of course, if you miss the spelling, you could ask one of your classmates after the class to spell the name for you, but I hope you did make some notation of the word so that you could go back later and fill in the spelling if you needed to. Let's see, look at your notes and see if you can identify what the speaker next talked about. I'll give you a number of words that should provide clues to the ideas presented by the lecturer: "buildings," "marketplaces, pyramid temples." Did you note down any of these words? Can you use these words (which you should have abbreviated) to construct a sentence about the capital city Tenochtitlan? (Pause.) Ok. The lecturer mentioned that human sacrifices were offered up on the pyramid temples. Who were the sacrificed victims? (Pause.) Yes, they were Indian prisoners of war. Let's go back to the lecture.

Some 300,000 people lived in the Aztec capital. It was, in fact, one of the largest cities in the sixteenth century world. It was five times larger than sixteenth-century London. The Aztecs were fierce fighters and the capital city of their empire was indeed a military fortress filled with soldiers. You know, the military intelligence system of the empire was so amazingly effective that their leader Montezuma knew that strange men—the Spaniards—were approaching his capital city long before they were anywhere near it. He also knew exactly how the Spanish soldiers rode horses and how they fired guns. Montezuma, by the way, ruled between the years 1480 and 1520.

Did you note down the number of Aztecs who were living in the capital? What did the lecturer say about the size of the Aztec capital? Check your notes. The lecturer mentioned the phrase "military fortress." Did you catch that phrase? Can you reconstruct what the lecturer said about the military fortress? If you have a military fortress, you might also have a military intelligence system in your empire. Look at your notes, and describe what the military intelligence system of the empire told Montezuma. (Pause.) Ok. The lecturer threw in an aside. An aside is like a parenthesis in writing. It provides information that is of interest but is somewhat off the immediate topic of discussion. You'll be taking notes for a longer period of time now. So take down as much of the information as you can in note form, and we'll check how you did when the lecturer stops.

In spite of his early-warning system, an army of only 553 Spanish soldiers managed to conquer the most powerful, advanced militaristic empire of the New World. How, indeed, was this possible? Why did it happen? Let's go back a bit. . . .

In the spring of the year 1519, an Indian runner from the Gulf Coast area of the Aztec Empire gave a strange report to Montezuma. He said that he had seen two floating mountains—they were, of course, the Spanish ships—and that out of these floating mountains, strangely dressed men had come—these men were the Spanish soldiers. The Indian said that the men had beards and that their skin was very white. When the emperor heard this report, he nervously remembered the Aztec legend of the bearded, light-skinned god, Quetzalcoatl. According to the legend, this god was supposed to return to earth one day to claim his kingdom which was, at that time, the Aztec Empire. So, Montezuma mistakenly, but perhaps understandably, assumed that Hernan Cortes, the leader of the soldiers of Spain, was the expected god, Quetzalcoatl. So he offered no resistance whatsoever to the approaching Spaniard and his small army. Instead, he sent presents of gold and silver to the approaching conquistadors. He asked them politely to leave his empire, but when the Spaniards saw the presents of gold and silver, they were even more excited and determined to conquer this empire for Spain and, of course, to steal its gold and silver.

Take a rest for a minute and take a look at your notes. Were you able to make enough notations in English so that you could reconstruct the historical narrative? The lecturer began by mentioning that only 553 soldiers conquered the Aztec empire. He asked how it was possible for this to happen, and he asked why it happened. Did you use question marks in your notes? Did you, for example, write in your notes, "question mark 'possible' "? And "question mark 'why' "? These two questions alert you to the fact that the lecturer will proceed to tell you why it was possible that a small band of 553 Spanish soldiers could conquer an empire, and why it happened. I'd like to repeat this part of the lecture so you can clean up and fill out your notes. Listen and fill in any important information you missed so you can retell the narrative at a later time. In the spring of the year 1519, an Indian runner from the Gulf Coast area of the Aztec Empire gave a strange report to Montezuma. He said that he had seen two floating mountains—they were, of course, the Spanish ships—and that out of these floating mountains, strangely dressed men had come—these men were the Spanish soldiers. The Indian said that the men had beards and that their skin was very white. When the emperor heard this report, he nervously remembered the Aztec legend of the bearded, light-skinned god, Quetzalcoatl. According to the legend this god was supposed to return to earth one day to claim his kingdom which was, at that time, the Aztec Empire. So, Montezuma mistakenly, but perhaps understandably, assumed that Hernan Cortes, the leader of the soldiers of Spain, was the expected god, Quetzalcoatl. So he offered no resistance whatsoever to the approaching Spaniard and his small army. Instead, he sent presents of gold and silver to the approaching conquistadors. He asked them politely to leave his empire, but when the Spaniards saw the presents of gold and silver, they were even more excited and determined to conquer this empire for Spain and, of course, to steal its gold and silver. All right. You should have had enough time to take down sufficient notes on this section of the lecture. It's important that you try to capture the main ideas and not every single word said. It's simply not possible to write down every word. Just write down enough that you can reconstruct the gist or main idea and important details of the narrative. Let's go on with the lecture. Are you ready?

In November of 1519, the Spaniards entered the capital city and took the Emperor Montezuma prisoner. It was not until June of 1520 that the Aztecs rebelled against the small army of Spaniards. Montezuma was killed during this rebellion. He was, so the story goes, stoned to death by his own people, but no one really knows whether it was the Spaniards or the Aztecs who caused Montezuma's death. Many Spanish soldiers were killed on what had been named *la noche triste*—"the sorrowful night"—which occurred on June 30 in 1520.

Cortes, who had been away from the capital at the start of the uprising, returned and attacked the city. According to Cortes's own figures, on one day of fighting for the capture of the Aztec capital, 40,000 Aztecs died; on another 12,000 were killed; and on another day of the battle 6,000 were killed by Spanish guns. The Indians, you see, were fighting with clubs and spears; the Spaniards with guns. The battle went on for seventy-five days, and finally on August 31, 1520 the greatest city of the Aztec Empire fell and was completely destroyed. Cortes founded Mexico City on its ruins.

Again, the question arises: How could an expedition of only 553 Spaniards manage to conquer the most powerful, war-like empire of the New World? Well, as I already mentioned, the prophecy of a returning god completely immobilized the leader of the empire. Montezuma didn't know exactly what to do as he awaited the arrival of what he thought was a god.

Furthermore, this god was accompanied by an army of gods who could fire flashes of lightning. (Remember, the Aztecs had never seen guns.) To make matters worse, the gods seemed to be half man and half animal. (The Spaniards rode on horses—the Aztecs had also never seen horses before.) To the Indians, the Spaniards must have looked like what men from Mars would look like to us today!

This time, I'm going to give you less help with your notes. You'll have to learn to rely on your own ability to listen and encode information in note form as you work through the material in Advanced Listening Comprehension, *but check your notes and see if you have notations that refer to the following pieces of information:*

November 1519. . . . What happened? What words or notations did you write down next to 1519? Did you make note of several key pieces of information: "floating mountains"? Maybe you missed the word "floating" and maybe you didn't understand this term "floating mountains" the first time you heard it, but even if you noted down the word incorrectly, you could return to your notes and clean up your notes after the lecture was over. How did the runner describe the strange men who came out of the floating mountains? Look in your notes. Did you note down any descriptive words? Did you abbreviate them? I'm sure there was no time to write down "white skin," so you could have written down "wh" or even "w," and "sk." As long as you can understand your notations, that's fine. Can you find in your notes the answer to the question "Why did Montezuma offer no resistance whatsoever to Cortes as he approached the empire? What did the lecturer say about Montezuma's "polite" request to Cortes? And finally, I'm sure you remember that Montezuma offered the Spaniards gold and silver as presents? What was the effect on the Spaniards? Ok, perhaps you remember what the effect was, and my question is "Did you need to take down the effect in your notes"? It's important, as I said earlier, not to write everything down, and if you can remember the effect, then you may not need to commit the idea to your notes. Fine. Let's finish up the lecture. This time, you will not be interrupted in your notetaking and you won't have me checking your comprehension and notetaking. At the end of the notetaking exercise, you should look over your notes and ask one of your classmates or your teacher to listen as you reconstruct the last part of the lecture from your notes. Let's get started.

Another important factor in the Aztecs' conquest was Cortes's use of Indian allies. He used Indian against Indian, so to speak. Cortes convinced the various Indian tribes to ally themselves with him against their hated enemies, the Aztecs. So, all along his march from the sea, Cortes gathered Indian allies until his small expedition of 553 Spanish adventurers increased to an army of over 75,000 fighting men. His success in gathering Indian allies was largely due to an Indian woman known as La Malinche. That's spelled L-a M-a-l-i-n-c-h-e. La Malinche, who was also called Doña Marina, spoke the languages of both the Aztec and Mayan Indians. As a result, Cortes, through her, could communicate in the two major Indian languages. So, she was a great help to Cortes in his negotiations with the Indians and even with the emperor Montezuma himself. In effect, she helped bring about the fall of the Aztec Empire.

And so we can perhaps sum up some of the major factors involved in the conquest of one of the greatest empires ever known. Well, to begin with, I'll cite man's fear of the supernatural—the fear of the appearance of a legendary god; second, let me cite the Spaniards' military superiority in the area of weapons—Spanish guns as opposed to Indian clubs; third, the tool of political intrigue—the turning of Indian against Indian; and last, but certainly not of least importance, the human thirst for adventure and the factor of human greed—the conquistadors were seeking gold and silver, and they did not care in the least if an empire and a culture were completely destroyed to satisfy their greed. All these factors and some others not even touched upon here led to the downfall of the mighty Aztec Empire. And yet, after its fall, another nation emerged, one which turned out to be a fusion of Indian and European culture. This cultural fusion eventually led to the overthrow of colonial rule and to the establishment of the Republic of Mexico.

LECTURE 2
THE EGYPTIAN PYRAMIDS: HOUSES OF ETERNITY

ORIENTATION LISTENING SCRIPT

To many people throughout the world, some of the most remarkable and puzzling monuments of ancient times are the pyramids of ancient Egypt. You know, almost nothing at all remains of the once-great cities of the kings of Egypt, the pharoahs. Time and weather have been hard on ancient Egypt's cities and towns, but several of the temples, statues, and, most important of all, the pyramids have survived. Even though many of the pyramids are in ruins, they still give us some idea of the magnificence of ancient Egypt's civilization—a civilization that, after all, lasted for more than 3,000 years. Remember when we're talking about ancient Egypt, we're talking about at least 30 consecutive dynasties. A dynasty is a series of kings or queens of the same royal family—something like the Romanovs of Europe, the Ming dynasty of China, or the Al-Sauds of Saudi Arabia.

As many of you probably already know, the pyramids were constructed as tombs or burial places for the Egyptian kings and their family members. You see, the ancient Egyptians passionately believed in life after death. In fact, their entire culture revolved around that belief. The kings, queens, and state officials often spent an entire lifetime preparing for their life after death. They did this by collecting possessions or "grave goods," by building tombs, and so forth. The Egyptians believed that they could be assured of an afterlife only if their bodies could be preserved from decay or destruction. So when a person died, and especially when a pharaoh died, in order to ensure his eternal life, he had his body embalmed or mummified. In other words, he had his corpse dried out and wrapped in linen to preserve it from decay. Then he had his mummy hidden. This whole idea may seem quite strange today, but the ancient Egyptians really believed that if one's mummy was destroyed, then his or her soul would be destroyed. And if, on the other hand, the mummy—the dead body—was preserved, the soul would be immortal. Let me repeat that. If one's mummy was preserved, the soul would go on living.

For another thing, the ancient Egyptians believed that the dead person could take his or her earthly possessions along to the next world—this is just the opposite of the Western idea that "you can't take it with you when you go." Anyway, the dead person was provided with food, clothing, furniture, weapons, and even servants. It was not at all unusual for the pharaoh's slaves to be put to death so that they could serve him in his afterlife.

So you can see why the pharaohs wanted to have their bodies and their possessions hidden to protect them from grave robbers. Before they died, they had special tombs built for this purpose—to hide their bodies and their treasures. In the early years of ancient Egypt, these tombs were the pyramids—the vast burial chambers that were built to fool the grave robbers. Unfortunately, the grave robbers almost always outsmarted even the most powerful and the most careful of pharaohs. They broke into most of the pyramids or tombs and stole the food and other treasures that they found. They even desecrated and destroyed the mummies of the dead. Needless to say, they would not bother a poor person's grave. These grave robbers even banded together into organizations or brotherhoods. Just imagine, a grave robbers' union!

Now, as for the actual construction of the mighty pyramids, it was during the First and Second Dynasties that the kings and nobles of Egypt began to construct the type of tomb called the "mastaba." The First and Second Dynasties lasted from about 3100 until 2665 B.C. Mastaba, by the way, comes from an Arabic word meaning "bench" or "long seat." A mastaba looked like a low, flat-topped rectangle—something like a low bench or a shoebox. Essentially, the pointed pyramid was no more than the extension upwards of the the flat-topped mastaba.

The first "typical" pyramid (or, at least what most people generally think a pyramid looks like) was built during the Third Dynasty, which lasted roughly from about 2664 until 2615 B.C. This pyramid was for King Zoser (that's spelled Z-o-s-e-r) in about 2650 B.C. It was built by an architect named Imhotep (I-m-h-o-t-e-p). This pyramid was constructed as a series of giant steps or stairs. It, along with the others of its type, is called the "step pyramid." It was really simply a pile of mastabas, each step smaller and higher than the one before. The step pyramid of King Zoser was different from the later pyramids because it was never covered with stone to give it a smooth surface.

Actually, it was not until the Fourth Dynasty that the most famous pyramids were built. The three Great Pyramids of Giza belong to the Fourth Dynasty pyramids. (The Fourth Dynasty covered the period from 2614 to 2502 B.C.) They are located near the town of Giza, on the west bank of the Nile River, just outside the capital city of Egypt, Cairo. The Great Pyramids are really the best preserved of all the Egyptian pyramids. The largest of these pyramids is known as the Great Pyramid. And great it is! It was built for King Khufu (that's K-h-u-f-u. Khufu was called Cheops—C-h-e-o-p-s —by the Greeks, and so the pryamid is sometimes called the Pyramid of Cheops.) It has been estimated that 2,300,000 blocks of limestone were used to build the Great Pyramid. The blocks averaged 2,500 kilos each. The largest stone block weighs about 15,000 kilos. The base of the pyramid covers 5.3 hectares—an area large enough to hold ten football fields. There's a story that the conqueror Napoleon once sat in the shadow of the Great Pyramid and calculated that the mass of stone in the pyramid could be used to build a wall three meters high by 0.3 meters thick around the entire country of France. In terms of height, the pyramid was originally 147 meters high, but today the top ten meters are missing, and the entire outer limestone covering had been stripped away. It seems that local builders and conquerors found it convenient to strip off the limestone from the pyramids and use it to build with.

The Great Pyramid of Khufu is considered a wonder of ancient architecture. When you look at it, you immediately wonder how on earth the ancient Egyptians ever managed to build such a structure with only basic mathematics; they had no modern machinery, such as cranes and bulldozers, and no iron tools. They had to cut the big limestone blocks with tools made of copper, which is a rather soft metal. But they managed to do it. The ancient Greek historian, Herodotus (that's H-e-r-o-d-o-t-u-s) said that 400,000 men worked for twenty years to build the Great Pyramid. Archeologists today doubt these figures, but, of course, the true statistics cannot ever really be determined. It is thought, though, that at least 100,000 worked to build any single pyramid. Most of these were slaves. They worked on the tombs during times when the Nile River overflowed its banks and covered the fields. The Nile's flooding made farming impossible and made transportation of the stone to the pyramid site easier.

The Second and Third Pyramids of Giza were built by Khufu's successors. The tomb of Khafre is the Second Pyramid of Giza. (Khafre is spelled K-h-a-f-r-e.) It was originally 3 meters lower than the Great Pyramid; however, today it is only 0.8 meters lower. Its present height is 136.2 meters.

The Third Pyramid, built for Menkaure, covers only half the area occupied by the Great Pyramid, and it is only 62.5 meters high. (Menkaure is spelled M-e-n-k-a-u-r-e.)

None of the later pyramids that were built during the next 13 or 14 centuries were nearly as large or as magnificent as the Pyramids of Giza. And even though pyramid building continued right up into the Eleventh and Twelfth Dynasties (that was up through about 1786 B.C.), it was becoming increasingly clear to the pharaohs and the nobles of Egypt that the pyramid method of burial provided really little or no protection at all for their royal corpses. The pyramids were, of course, impressive and lasting monuments, but they were all too visible. They invited grave robbers to try to break into them. And so eventually, one of the pharaohs, King Thutmose I, decided to sacrifice publicity for safety in the construction of his House of Eternity. (I don't need to spell Thutmose for you, do I?) Instead of ordering the construction of a pyramid, Thutmose had his tomb dug out of the rock of a valley far from the Nile River and far from Cairo. The spot he chose was some 11 kilometers from the river on its west bank. The area is now known as the Valley of the Kings. Many pharaohs followed Thutmose's example. After him, most of the pharaohs abandoned above-ground pyramid construction in favor of underground hiding places as the burial places for their precious royal bones. And yet, what is so ironic is that even these tombs did not escape the attacks of the grave robbers—persistent devils that they were!

I'll end this discussion by pointing out that, when the ancient Greeks first saw the Great Pyramids of Egypt, the pyramids were already 2,000 years old. The Greeks called them one of the Seven Wonders of the World. Almost nothing remains of the other six Wonders—the Hanging Gardens of Babylon, the Temple of Diana, and so on—but the three mighty Pyramids of Giza, as well as 32 other recognizable pyramids, still stand. These pyramids of Egypt are monuments to a great and ancient civilization and to people's endless search for eternal recognition and eternal life.

LISTENING AND NOTETAKING SCRIPT

To many people throughout the world, some of the most remarkable and puzzling monuments of ancient times are the pyramids of ancient Egypt. You know, almost nothing at all remains of the once-great cities of the kings of Egypt, the pharaohs. Time and weather have been really hard on ancient Egypt's cities and towns, but several of the temples, statues, and, most important of all, the pyramids have survived. Even though many of the pyramids are in ruins, they still give us some idea of the magnificence of ancient Egypt's civilization—a civilization that, after all, lasted for more than 3,000 years. Remember when we're talking about ancient Egypt, we're talking about at least thirty consecutive dynasties. A dynasty is a series of kings or queens of the same royal family—something like the Romanovs of Europe, the Ming dynasty of China, or the Al-Sauds of Saudi Arabia.

Ok. The introduction to the lecture was just that . . . An introduction to the general topic of the lecture, the remarkable pyramids of Egypt. The lecturer notes that almost nothing remains of the once-great cities of Egypt because time and weather have been hard on the cities, but the great pyramids have survived, though many are in ruins. The lecturer did mention how long the civilization of Egypt lasted. Did you note down the figure? Did you also note down how many dynasties or royal families ruled for the 3,000 years mentioned? I wonder if you felt the need to write down in your notes the names of the famous dynasties the lecturer mentioned. Why or why not? In a sentence can you sum up the introductory message of the lecture?

Let's continue taking notes. The lecturer open this part of the lecture with an evident fact—that the pyramids were constructed as tombs. You might want to abbreviate the word "tomb" with the letter "t" and every time you hear the lecturer mention information about tombs in this lecture, you can use the letter "t" to save you notetaking time. You'll be taking notes for a longer period of time now, so try to capture the ideas and the details so you can reconstruct the information you hear at a later time.

As many of you probably already know, the pyramids were constructed as tombs or burial places for the Egyptian kings and their family members. You see, the ancient Egyptians passionately believed in life after death. In fact, their entire culture revolved around that belief. The kings, queens, and state officials often spent an entire lifetime preparing for their life after death. They did this by collecting possessions or "grave goods," by building tombs, and so forth. The Egyptians believed that they could be assured of an afterlife only if their bodies could be preserved from decay or destruction. So when a person died, and especially when a pharaoh died, in order to ensure his eternal life, he had his body embalmed or mummified. In other words, he had his corpse dried out and wrapped in linen to preserve it from decay. Then he had his mummy hidden. This whole idea may seem quite strange today, but the ancient Egyptians really believed that if one's mummy was destroyed, then his or her soul would be destroyed, and if, on the other hand, the mummy—the dead body—was preserved, the soul would be immortal. Let me repeat that. If one's mummy was preserved, the soul would go on living.

For another thing, the ancient Egyptians believed that the dead person could take his or her earthly possessions along to the next world—this is just the opposite of the Western idea that "you can't take it with you when you go." Anyway, the dead person was provided with food, clothing, furniture, weapons, and even servants. It was not at all unusual for the pharaoh's slaves to be put to death so that they could serve him in his afterlife.

And so you can see why the pharaohs wanted to have their bodies and their possessions hidden to protect them from grave robbers. Before they died, they had special tombs built for this purpose—to hide their bodies and their treasures. In the early years of ancient Egypt, these tombs were the pyramids—the vast burial chambers that were built to fool the grave robbers. Unfortunately, the grave robbers almost always outsmarted even the most powerful and the most careful of pharaohs. They broke into most of the pyramids or tombs and stole the food and other treasures that they found. They even desecrated and destroyed the mummies of the dead. Needless to say, they would not bother a poor person's grave. These grave robbers even banded together into organizations or brotherhoods. Just imagine, a grave robbers' union!

I'm going to give you an outline of the information in this section of the lecture. Look at your notes. Did you attempt to organize the information in outline form? You may not have gotten too far in doing it the first time you take your notes, but if you can make an outline that is meaningful to you while you're listening, you can go back later and make a more formal outline of the information when you have a chance to fill in more information.

Ok. The pyramids were constructed as burial places for the ancient Egyptian royal family members. What notations (or abbreviations) did you need to make in your notes to be able to reconstruct this idea? It will, no doubt, vary with individual notetakers. Each of us takes notes differently, and remember we only need to interpret the notes for ourselves, so you can develop a system that works for you. But this is an aside. I'll get back to the outline of the critical pieces of information in the lecture. Ok. The ancient Egyptians believed in life after death. As a result, they prepared for their afterlife by building tomb and by collecting possessions or "grave goods" for their tombs. The Egyptians believed that they could be assured of an afterlife only if their bodies could be preserved from decay or destruction. To ensure eternal life, the pharaohs had their bodies embalmed or mummified. If one's mummy was destroyed, then the soul would be destroyed. The Egyptians had another belief; they believed they could take their earthly possessions along to the next world. They could take food, clothing, furniture, weapons, and even servants. And you know what happened to some of the Pharaoh's servants when he died, right? But the rich and powerful pharaohs didn't couldn't keep their bodies and treasures safe from a certain group of people.

Who were they? What did the lecturer say about a grave robbers' union? Let's return to the lecture and listen as the lecturer describes the evolution of the pyramid structure. You will listen to a number of facts and figures in this part of the lecture. You'll need to listen carefully and write down the dates the lecturer gives on the dynasties. Are you ready to take some notes?

As for the actual construction of the mighty pyramids, it was during the First and Second Dynasties that the kings and nobles of Egypt began to construct the type of tomb called "the mastaba." The First and Second Dynasties lasted from about 3100 until 2665 B.C. Mastaba, by the way, comes from an Arabic word meaning "bench" or "long seat." A mastaba looked like a low, flat-topped rectangle—something like a low bench or a shoebox. Essentially, the pointed pyramid was no more than the extension upwards of the flat-topped mastaba.

The first "typical" pyramid (or, at least what most people generally think a pyramid looks like) was built during the Third Dynasty (which lasted roughly from about 2664 until 2615 B.C.) This pyramid was for King Zoser (that's spelled Z-o-s-e-r) in about 2650 B.C. It was built by an architect named Imhotep (I-m-h-o-t-e-p). This pyramid was constructed as a series of giant steps or stairs. It, along with the others of its type, is called the Step Pyramid. It was really simply a pile of mastabas, each higher step smaller than the one before. The Step Pyramid of King Zoser was different from the later pyramids because it was never covered with stone to give it a smooth surface.

Ok, check your notes. What was the first type of pyramid constructed and when was it begun? Right. It was during the First and Second Dynasties that the kings and nobles of Egypt began to construct the type of tomb called "the mastaba." How long did the First and Second Dynasties last? From about 3100 until 2665 B.C. The lecturer defined the Arabic word "mastaba." What did you write down in your notes? You could have drawn pictures of a low bench or a shoe box and then drawn a picture with the bench extended upward into a mastaba. Notes don't and can't always be in word form. Illustrations work also in certain cases. Continuing. . . . The lecturer noted that the first "typical" pyramid was built during the Third Dynasty. How long did the Third Dynasty last? Let me ask some other questions: (1) Who was the first pyramid built for? Check your notes. (2) When was Zoser's pyramid built and (3) who built it? (4) What did it look like? If you got the information down in your notes, you should be able to answer all those questions. How did the Step Pyramid of King Zoser differ from the later pyramids? Check your notes? Ok. We'll return to the lecture and finish up our notetaking. The information won't be repeated after you hear it this time, so you'll have to listen carefully and work out a method for taking down the information in note form. Ready?

Actually, it was not until the Fourth Dynasty that the most famous pyramids were built. The three Great Pyramids of Giza belong to the Fourth Dynasty pyramids. (The Fourth Dynasty covered the period form 2614 to 2502 B.C.) They are located near the town of Giza, on the west bank of the Nile River, just outside the capital city of Egypt, Cairo. The Great Pyramids are really the very best preserved of all the Egyptian pyramids. The largest of these pyramids is known as the Great Pyramid. And great it is! It was built for King Khufu (that's K-h-u-f-u). (Khufu was called Cheops [C-h-e-o-p-s] by the Greeks, and so the pyramid is sometimes called the Pyramid of Cheops.) It has been estimated that 2,300,000 blocks of limestone were used to build the Great Pyramid. The blocks averaged 2,500 kilos each. The largest stone block weighs about 15,000 kilos. The base of the pyramid covers 5.3 hectares—an area large enough to hold ten football fields. There's a story that the conqueror Napoleon once sat in the shadow of the Great Pyramid and calculated that the mass of stone in the pyramid could be used to build a wall three meters high by 0.3 meters thick around the entire country of France. In terms of height, the pyramid was originally 147 meters high, but today the top ten meters are missing, and the entire outer limestone covering had been stripped away. It seems that local builders and conquerors found it convenient to strip off the limestone from the pyramids and use it to build with.

The Great Pyramid of Khufu is considered a wonder of ancient architecture. When you look at it, you immediately wonder how on earth the ancient Egyptians ever managed to build such a structure with only basic mathematics, with no modern machinery (such as cranes, bulldozers, and so forth), and with no iron tools. They had to cut the big limestone blocks with tools made of copper, which is a rather soft metal. But they did manage to do it. The ancient Greek historian, Herodotus (that's H-e-r-o-d-o-t-u-s)—Herodotus said that 400,000 men worked for twenty years to build the Great Pyramid. Archaeologists today doubt these figures, but, of course, the true statistics cannot ever really be determined. It is thought, though, that at least 100,000 worked to build any single pyramid. Most of these were slaves. They worked on the tombs during times when the Nile River overflowed its banks and covered the fields. The Nile's flooding made farming impossible and made transportation of the stone to the pyramid site easier.

The Second and Third Pyramids of Giza were built by Khufu's successors. The tomb of Khafre is the Second Pyramid of Giza. (Khafre is spelled K-h-a-f-r-e.) It was originally 3 meters lower than the Great Pyramid; however, today it is only 0.8 meters lower. Its present height is 136.2 meters.

The Third Pyramid, built for Menkaure, covers only half the area occupied by the Great Pyramid, and it is only 62.5 meters high. Menkaure is spelled M-e-n-k-a-u-r-e.

None of the later pyramids that were built during the next 13 or 14 centuries were nearly as large or as magnificent as the Pyramids of Giza. And even though pyramid building continued right up into the Eleventh and Twelfth Dynasties (that was up through about 1786 B.C.), it was becoming increasingly clear to the pharaohs and the nobles of Egypt that the pyramid method of burial provided really very little or no protection at all for their royal corpses. The pyramids were, of course, impressive and lasting monuments, but they were all too visible. They invited grave robbers to try to break into them. And so eventually, one of the pharaohs, King Thutmose I, decided to sacrifice publicity for safety in the construction of his House of Eternity. I don't need to spell Thutmose for you, do I? Instead of ordering the construction of a pyramid, Thutmose had his tomb dug out of the rock of a valley far from the Nile River and far from Cairo. The spot he chose was some 11 kilometers from the river on its west bank. The area is now known as the Valley of the Kings. Many pharaohs followed Thutmose's example.

After him, most of the pharaohs abandoned above-ground pyramid construction in favor of underground hiding places as the burial places for their precious royal bones. And yet, what is so ironic is that even these tombs did not escape the attacks of the grave robbers—persistent devils that they were!

I'll end this discussion by pointing out that, when the ancient Greeks first saw the Great Pyramids of Egypt, the pyramids were already 2,000 years old. The Greeks called them one of the Seven Wonders of the World. Almost nothing remains of the other six Wonders—the Hanging Gardens of Babylon, the Temple of Diana, and so on, but the three mighty Pyramids of Giza, as well as thirty-two other recognizable pyramids, still stand—monuments to a great and ancient civilization and to people's endless search for eternal recognition and eternal life.

Well, how did you do on your own with this part of the lecture? There was a great deal of information and you need to decide how much to write down and how much to rely on your memory. You'll be having an examination on the material, and you can use your notes to refresh your memory, but you still need to develop your own system for listening and taking notes on a lecture presentation. You'll have lots of practice by the time you finish this course of instruction.

Unit 2
Portraits of Political Leaders: Mystique Versus Reality

LECTURE 3
JOHN F. KENNEDY: PROMISE AND TRAGEDY

ORIENTATION LISTENING SCRIPT

It seems that John Fitzgerald Kennedy has been honored after his death as he never was during his life. Along with such men as George Washington, Abraham Lincoln, and Thomas Jefferson, he has been given a place in legend. Kennedy's murder in November of 1963—only two years and ten months after he became president—has become a symbol of the tragedy and senselessness of life.

Kennedy was quite a surprising person. He never did things when others were doing them. Let me give you a few examples of what I mean. He went to Congress and the White House earlier than most elected Presidents. He was only twenty-nine years old when he won his first political election in 1947. He was elected president of the United States when he was only forty-three years old. At the age of forty-six, he was assassinated. Yes, Kennedy was the youngest man ever to be elected president of the United States, and, sadly, he was the youngest man ever to die in that office. He was also the first American president born in the 1900s.

Although Kennedy was young, well-educated, and rich, things did not always go smoothly for him. He suffered a series of mishaps and tragedies during his life. Let me cite a few of these misfortunes. During World War II, he suffered a serious back injury. He had major surgery in 1954 and again in 1955 to correct the injury; however, his back bothered him for the rest of his life. While he was president, his son died soon after birth. His life was a mixture of political triumph and personal misfortune.

To judge Kennedy's 1,000 days in the White House is not easy. One of the reasons is that for a man who had such a keen sense of history, he was really quite disorderly about keeping records of what influenced and led up to his own political decisions. It is said that he often made these decisions alone and after a series of private talks with his many advisers and with his younger brother, Robert Kennedy (who was also assassinated—in 1968). From the numerous accounts of the Kennedy years, it seems that none of these advisers actually took part in the whole process of Kennedy's decision making. Apparently he spent very little time talking even to his closest associates about how he made final decisions. As a result, we don't have the full story on the two Cuban crises—the disastrous invasion of the Bay of Pigs in 1961 and the Russian attempt to install missiles in Cuba in 1962. We also don't know why, during his administration, the United States became more and more deeply involved in the civil war in Vietnam. We don't even have all the background on what led up to the Atomic Test Ban Treaty of 1963. You may remember that under this treaty, the United States, England, and the U.S.S.R. agreed not to test any more nuclear weapons in the earth's atmosphere, in outer space, or under water. I guess we could say that Kennedy relied heavily on his own judgment in making policy decisions. Many of these decisions reflect Kennedy's idealism—and, sometimes his lack of realism.

In his handling of American foreign policy, for instance, Kennedy envisioned a strong, interdependent Atlantic world—that was his ideal—but the reality was something else. For example, the North Atlantic Treaty Organization (or NATO) was in rather poor shape during most of his administration. Only three years after Kennedy's death, France withdrew from the military affairs of NATO. In Latin America, he won admiration with his plans for the Alliance for Progress, but again, as any Latin American will tell you, the Alliance was much more a dream than a reality. One of his more successful idealistic plans was the creation of the Peace Corps, which was supposed to make American technical skills available to some of the developing countries.

But because of this idealism, his youth, and his personal charm, I think most people would agree on one thing. President Kennedy was a lot more effective in the world of international diplomacy than he ever was in the world of domestic politics. He enjoyed meeting with the heads of foreign countries and with foreign students at the White House, and he had a rare combination of informality and dignity that made him very effective in this role. But to make small-talk—to chit-chat—with self-important American congressmen really bored him, and he simply would not take the time to do it as his successor, President Lyndon Johnson, did with such political success. Kennedy and the American Congress did not get along very well. As a result, Kennedy had a great deal of difficulty getting his domestic programs approved by Congress. The "New Frontier," as his administration was called, had some successes in its first year. For example, Congress established the Peace Corps; Congress also raised the minimum wage from $1.00

to $1.25 per hour. (The minimum wage is the least amount of money per hour that a worker can legally be paid.) Today, by the way, the minimum wage is $4.25 per hour. Congress also increased Social Security benefits—which is money that is paid to people sixty-five years and older. Kennedy also succeeded in getting more money for space exploration programs. During his administration, American astronauts made their first space flights and began their preparation to send men to the moon. Just six years after Kennedy's death, the first man actually landed on the moon.

However, the Congress refused to pass many proposals that Kennedy suggested. The proposals failed, in other words. Let me list just a few of these proposals Congress refused to pass: (1) free medical care for people over sixty-five; (2) the creation of a Department of Urban Affairs—American cities were in a state of decay; (3) federal aid to education; and (4) tax reform and tax reduction. It's quite possible that, because the country was experiencing general prosperity, it was difficult to convince Congress or the American people of the need for serious social and political change in the U.S. When Kennedy was assassinated in 1963, his entire domestic program was in big trouble.

And yet, part of the Kennedy legend is connected with his introduction of the most radical legislation affecting the African Americans in the United States in this century. He was responsible for the bill that prohibited discrimination, in this case racial discrimination, in employment, and in public facilities such as public transportation, in restaurants, and restrooms, and so on. He was also responsible for the bill that outlawed school segregation. This bill, however, was passed by Congress, but not until after Kennedy's death.

Although the promise and tragedy of John F. Kennedy was, in many ways, a lot greater than any of his actual accomplishments, the tragedy of his death resulted in definite social reform in the United States, and it left the hope that a youthful, idealistic person like John Kennedy will appear on the American political scene, another president who will remind the American people to "ask not what your country can do for you; ask what you can do for your country."

LISTENING AND NOTETAKING SCRIPT

It seems that John Fitzgerald Kennedy has been honored after his death as he never was during his life. Along with such men as George Washington, Abraham Lincoln, and Thomas Jefferson, he has been given a place in legend. Kennedy's murder in November of 1963—only two years and ten months after he became president—has become a symbol of the tragedy and senselessness of life to many Americans.

The lecturer began with a very short introduction to the lecture and to the story of John Fitzgerald Kennedy. If you didn't write down Kennedy's middle name, don't worry. Did you catch the names of the other famous men the lecturer mentioned? Who were they? Look at your notes. The lecturer mentioned the names of Washington, Lincoln, and Thomas Jefferson. Finally, the lecturer mentioned that Kennedy was murdered in November 1963—two years and ten months after he became president. His death is viewed as a symbol of tragedy to many Americans. Let's return to the task of listening and taking lecture notes. Listen carefully and write down what you can as you listen.

Kennedy was quite a surprising person. He never did things when others were doing them. Let me give you a few examples of what I mean. He went to Congress and the White House earlier than most elected presidents. He was only twenty-nine years old when he won his first political election in 1947. He was elected president of the United States when he was only forty-three years old. At the age of forty-six, he was assassinated. Yes, Kennedy was the youngest man ever to be elected president of the United States, and, sadly, he was the youngest man ever to die in that office. He was also the first American president born in the 1900s.

The lecturer begins with the statement that Kennedy was quite a surprising person. Did you note the examples he gave to document this statement? Did you begin to think of making a list of examples in your notes? Let's see. He mentioned that Kennedy went to Congress and the White House earlier than most elected Presidents. Did you write down that he was 29 years old? Did you note down the numbers 43 and 46? What do these numbers refer to? Finally, the lecturer mentioned that Kennedy was the youngest man to be elected president, and. . . . What else? (Pause.) Fine. Let's continue. This time, you'll take notes for a longer stretch of the lecture. The lecturer mentions a number of dates in the next segment of the lecture. Be sure to write down why these dates are important. Are you ready?

Although Kennedy was young, well-educated, and rich, things did not always go smoothly for him. He suffered a series of mishaps and tragedies during his life. Let me cite a few of these misfortunes. During World War II, he suffered a serious back injury. He had major surgery in 1954 and again in 1955 to correct the injury; however, his back bothered him for the rest of his life. While he was president, his son died soon after birth. His life was a mixture of political triumph and personal misfortune.

To judge Kennedy's 1,000 days in the White House is not easy. One of the reasons is that for a man who had such a keen sense of history, he was really quite disorderly about keeping records of what influenced and led up to his own political decisions. It is said that he often made these decisions alone and after a series of private talks with his many advisers and with his younger brother, Robert Kennedy (who was also assassinated—in 1968). From the numerous accounts of the Kennedy years, it seems that none of these advisers actually took part in the whole process of Kennedy's decision making. Apparently he spent very little time talking even to his closest associates about how he made final decisions. As a result, we don't have the full story on the two Cuban crises—the disastrous invasion of the Bay of Pigs in 1961 and the Russian attempt to install missiles in Cuba in 1962. We also don't know why, during his administration, the United States became more and more deeply involved in the civil war in Vietnam. We don't even have all the background on what led up to the Atomic Test Ban Treaty of 1963. You may remember that under this treaty, the United States, England, and the U.S.S.R. agreed not to test any more nuclear weapons in the earth's atmosphere, in outer space, or under water. I guess we could say that Kennedy relied heavily on his own judgment in making policy decisions. Many of these decisions reflect Kennedy's idealism—and, sometimes his lack of realism.

Take a moment to catch your breath and to examine your notes. The lecturer began talking about Kennedy's good fortune and bad fortune. He said Kennedy was young, well-educated, and rich. That's the good fortune part. How did you note this bit of information down? Did you write down the words "young," "well-educated," "rich"? Then he mentioned the bad fortune part. What did he say about that? (Pause.) Did you use your memory to answer this question or your notes? Or both? The lecturer listed some of the tragedies in JFK's life: a back injury in the war; surgery which was not that successful in 1954 and 1955; the death of his son soon after birth. You could synthesize all this information in two phrases the lecturer used: "political triumph" and "personal misfortune." I'll now ask you to review your notes on the segment of the lecture in which the speaker talks about judging Kennedy's 1,000 days in the White House. He mentioned several things about Kennedy's decision-making strategy and whose advice he took. He— and many people—have questions about how JFK made final decisions about the following issues: (1) the Bay of Pigs invasion of Cuba in 1961; (2) the Russian attempt to install missiles in Cuba in 1962; (3) U.S. involvement in the civil war in Vietnam; and (4) the Atomic Test Ban Treaty. The lecturer says Kennedy—and I quote—"relied heavily on his own judgment in making policy decisions." How could you shorten this idea into a few notations or words? Did you write down "own judgment"—abbreviated, of course— and "policy decisions"? What did the lecturer say about Kennedy's "idealism" and his "lack of realism"? In the next part of the lecture, the speaker explains what he meant. Let's listen and continue taking notes.

In his handling of American foreign policy, for instance, Kennedy envisioned a strong, interdependent Atlantic world—that was his ideal—but the reality was something else. For example, the North Atlantic Treaty Organization (or NATO) was in rather poor shape during most of his administration. Only three years after Kennedy's death, France withdrew from the military affairs of NATO. In Latin America, he won admiration with his plans for the Alliance for Progress, but again, as any Latin American will tell you, the Alliance was much more a dream than a reality. One of his more successful idealistic plans was the creation of the Peace Corps, which was supposed to make American technical skills available to some of the developing countries.

I'll ask you to rely on your developing ability to listen and take notes by not reviewing each piece of information presented in this short segment of the lecture. I'll simply point out some of the important words and phrases about Kennedy's vision and the reality of that vision. I hope you noted many, if not all of the words and phrases. You might have used columns in your notes or dashes to distinguish the ideal versus the reality:

- *the vision: strong, independent NATO; the reality: NATO in poor shape.*
- *the vision: the plan for the Alliance for Progress; the reality: the Alliance was a dream.*
- *the vision: the Peace Corps—perhaps the only plan that was both vision and reality for some developing countries.*

Ok. Let's continue as the lecturer discusses Kennedy the successful international diplomat versus Kennedy the less successful domestic politician. The lecturer will continue for a longer amount of time, and you need to begin to depend on your power to listen and note down information the first time you hear it. Are you ready?

But because of this idealism, his youth, and his personal charm, I think most people would agree on one thing. President Kennedy was a lot more effective in the world of international diplomacy than he ever was in the world of domestic politics. He enjoyed meeting with the heads of foreign countries and with foreign students at the White House, and he had a rare combination of informality and dignity that made him very effective in this role. But to make small-talk—to chit-chat—with self-important American congressmen really bored him, and he simply would not take the time to do it as his successor, President Lyndon Johnson, did with such political success. Kennedy and the American Congress did not get along very well. As a result, Kennedy had a great deal of difficulty getting his domestic programs approved by Congress. The "New Frontier," as his administration was called, had some successes in its first year. For example, Congress established the Peace Corps; Congress also raised the minimum wage from $1.00 to $1.25 per hour. (The minimum wage is the least amount of money per hour that a worker can legally be paid.) Today, by the way, the minimum wage is $4.25 per hour. Congress also increased Social Security benefits— which is money that is paid to people sixty-five years and older. Kennedy also succeeded in getting more money for space exploration programs. During his administration, American astronauts made their first space flights and began their preparation to send men to the moon. Just six years after Kennedy's death, the first man actually landed on the moon.

However, the Congress refused to pass many proposals that Kennedy suggested. The proposals failed, in other words. Let me list just a few of these proposals Congress refused to pass: (1) free medical care for people over sixty-five; (2) the creation of a Department of Urban Affairs—American cities were in a state of decay; (3) federal aid to education; and (4) tax reform and tax reduction. It's quite possible that, because the country was experiencing general prosperity, it was difficult to convince Congress or the American people of the need for serious social and political change in the U.S. When Kennedy was assassinated in 1963, his entire domestic program was in big trouble.

And yet, part of the Kennedy legend is connected with his introduction of the most radical legislation affecting the African Americans in the United States in this century. He was responsible for the bill that prohibited discrimination, in this case racial discrimination, in employment, and in public facilities such as public transportation, in restaurants, and restrooms, and so on. He was also responsible for the bill that outlawed school segregation. This bill, however, was passed by Congress, but not until after Kennedy's death.

Let's check your notes on this section of the lecture. I'll list some of the main points mentioned and you check your notes to see whether you can reconstruct the information from your notes.

Did you write down key words that would allow you to talk about Kennedy's effectiveness in the world of international diplomacy? Look at your notes to see whether or not you noted the following information about his domestic programs:

- *the creation of the Peace Corps?*
- *the increase of social benefits?*
- *support for space flights?*

Did you note down the failures in Kennedy's domestic programs involving:

- *free medical care for people over 65?*
- *creation of a Department of Urban Affairs for America's cities?*
- *federal aid to education?*
- *tax reform and tax reduction?*
- *the legislation affecting African Americans?*

That was a tremendous amount of information to take in and take down in note form. Let's finish up the lecture with just a few words about the promise and tragedy of John F. Kennedy.

Although the promise and tragedy of John F. Kennedy was, in many ways, a lot greater than any of his actual accomplishments, the tragedy of his death resulted in definite social reform in the United States, and it left the hope that a youthful, idealistic person like John Kennedy will appear on the American political scene, another president who will remind the American people to "ask not what your country can do for you; ask what you can do for your country."

LECTURE 4
INDIRA GANDHI: A SAD SONG OF INDIA

ORIENTATION LISTENING SCRIPT

Assassination is a most unfortunate experience for two famous families to have in common, but sadly, it is one shared by the Gandhi and the Kennedy families. Like the Kennedy brothers, John and Robert Kennedy, Indira and her son Rajiv were political victims. The mother was struck down by internal extremists in 1984. Her son was assassinated in 1991. I would like to dwell, however, not on the death of Indira Ghandi, but on the woman herself. In my brief talk, I will try to capture something of the problems she faced and something of the essential character of Indira Gandhi, which, depending on the circumstance, appeared to be brave, imperious, and to many, a bit disdainful of the concerns of ordinary mortals. To illustrate my point, it is reported that a day or two before her death she said to a friend who was worried about her personal safety, "Assassination is a risk you have to take. In politics you simply can't hide from people. My life has been one with India, and it makes no difference to me if I die standing or in bed."

To the surprise of many people, neither Indira nor her husband, Feroze Gandhi, was related to Mahatma Gandhi, the foremost political and spiritual leader in India in the twentieth century. She was, furthermore, the daughter of Jawaharlal Nehru, a follower of Mahatma Gandhi and himself a world-respected statesman. Nehru became India's first prime minister in 1947.

Gandhi was born in central India in 1917. She attended Santiniketan University before going to Oxford University in England. In 1942, she married Feroze Gandhi and had two sons, Rajiv and Sanjay. She suffered the death of her husband, Feroze and one of her sons before she herself was killed. Her husband died in 1960, and her son Sanjay was killed in an airplane crash in 1980. Both Kennedy and Ghandi suffered the loss of a son in their lifetimes, and both experienced the loss of loved ones in airplane crashes. The Kennedy family lost two members in crashes, Joseph Jr. and Kathleen, in the 1940s. Loss and death visited both the Ghandi and Kennedy families.

Gandhi began her political career as an adviser to her father Nehru. Later she herself was elected to Parliament in 1964. That same year she became Minister of Information and Broadcasting until she was chosen prime minister in 1966. She held the office of Minister of Information and Broadcasting for eleven years. In 1975, she was found guilty of illegal practices during the parliamentary election campaign of 1971. In spite of pressure to resign her Ministry office, she refused to do so. Instead of resigning, she declared a national emergency and had a number of her major opponents arrested. This turned out to be one of the biggest mistakes of her political career. Later that same year, her conviction was overturned by India's Supreme Court. Despite the fact that her conviction was overturned, when parliamentary elections were held in 1977, Indira Gandhi's Congress Party was defeated. With the defeat of the Congress Party, she lost both her position as prime minister and her seat in the Parliament. Actually, she was defeated by the party that, Morarji Desai, one of her long-time enemies, had formed just hours after he was released from prison. (Gandhi had sent him to prison.) This setback—this loss of her seat in Parliament—prompted her to organize a new "Congress-I" Party. The I, of course, stood for "Indira." In 1980, her new party gained control of Parliament and she once again became prime minister. She held the post of prime minister until her death four years later in 1984.

Throughout both her first and second terms as prime minister, she continued to lose popularity and the support of a large section of her own Congress Party. What were some of the reasons?

Remember, Gandhi was a Brahmin, a Hindu of the highest caste in India; she was privileged, aristocratic, and willful. She had a lonely childhood, a situation not unusual for a daughter of a famous and busy father, and she learned to rely heavily on herself, often giving the impression that because of her aristocratic heritage, she felt that she could do no wrong. She often demonstrated that she believed she could do no wrong when dealing with political issues and conflict situations in one of the most complex countries in the world. When Gandhi took office, for example, there was widespread unrest throughout the country because of food shortages, gross unemployment, the country's involvement in a disastrous civil war with Pakistan, and other problems too numerous to mention. At the same time, along with the United States and the former Soviet Union, India was becoming a player in the world atomic chess game by testing its first atomic bomb. India's testing of the atomic bomb caused worldwide concern—to put it mildly.

Gandhi experienced political setback, and had major personal and political troubles during her term as prime minister. But what were the major strengths of this woman who rose to the heights of power in India? Throughout her long and inconsistent political career, she worked ceaselessly to build up India's stature and place among the powerful nations of the world. She struggled to enlarge and expand India's autonomy in the areas of politics, economics, science, technology, and culture. Most likely, her greatest service to India was to preserve its unity as a nation. And that she did. Today, some of her biographers fear that this contribution is being completely forgotten or downplayed.

Gandhi's murder was undoubtedly the result of great friction between India's Sikh religious group and the ruling government. Her murder prompted numerous acts of violence against the Sikh minorities throughout the country. At the time, her assassination was often described as an act of pure and pointless vengeance. But it should be noted that from the Sikh point of view, the attack on Mrs. Gandhi was not without some provocation. Throughout the years, and especially under Mrs. Gandhi, the Sikhs had faced systematic discrimination. Despite their impressive martial tradition, they were kept out of the army even though roughly thirty percent of the officers were Sikhs. The state had taken precious water rights from Sikh farmers, and India's nationalized banks would not invest in areas where Sikhs lived. In June of 1984, according to an official report, her government ordered the Indian army to attack a group of Sikh extremists who had occupied the Sikh Golden Temple in Amaritsar in north central India. Six hundred and fifty people were killed, including government soldiers. One Sikh observer explaining the violation of the Holy Shrine said, "You cannot begin to understand our reactions unless you think in terms of the Vatican being besieged and overrun by storm troopers."

What followed the shooting of Indira Gandhi was strangely familiar to anyone who had witnessed the Kennedy assassination in 1963. There was a struggle with the two assailants who shot the prime minister. In the struggle, one of the assailants was killed; the other was critically wounded. There was a frantic rush of the prime minister to the hospital, followed by the fruitless attempts of desperate surgeons to save the life of the political leader of the country. After the doctors failed to save the 66-year-old prime minister, her passing was announced with the simple statement: "She is no more."

Immediately after her death—in fact, the same day as her assassination—the Congress-I Party chose her son Rajiv as its head. Thus, he succeeded his mother as prime minister and served in that office until 1989. Two years later Rajiv, too, was murdered while campaigning for a parliament seat.

In total, the Gandhi family had governed India for 32 of the 37 years since its independence. The relatives of John and Robert Kennedy are also still involved in American politics, more than 30 years after John Kennedy became president of the United States. The difficulty of governing millions of people fairly and democratically, whether in the United States or India, is becoming increasingly evident as countries in the world become more and more complex in terms of their social, political, economic, and religious diversity.

LISTENING AND NOTETAKING SCRIPT

Assassination is a most unfortunate experience for two famous families to have in common, but sadly, it is one shared by the Gandhi and the Kennedy families. Like the Kennedy brothers, John and Robert Kennedy,

Indira and her son Rajiv were both political victims. The mother was struck down by internal extremists in 1984. Her son was assassinated in 1991. I would like to dwell, however, not on the death of Indira Ghandi, but on the woman herself. In my brief talk, I will try to capture something of the problems she faced and something of the essential character of Indira Gandhi, which, depending on the circumstance, appeared to be brave, imperious, and to many, a bit disdainful of the concerns of ordinary mortals. To illustrate my point, it is reported that a day or two before her death she said to a friend who was worried about her personal safety, "Assassination is a risk you have to take. In politics you simply can't hide from people. My life has been one with India, and it makes no difference to me if I die standing or in bed."

Take a look at your notes. What did you write down of the introductory information provided by the lecturer? (Pause.) Using your notes, can you answer these questions? What did the lecturer say the Kennedys and the Gandhis had in common? (Pause.) What were the names of the victims? (Pause.) What happened in 1984? (Pause.) What happened in 1991? (Pause.) Next, the lecturer indicated that she would be talking less about the death of Gandhi and more about the character of Gandhi. How did she describe Gandhi? (Pause.) Let's return to the lecture.

To the surprise of many people, neither Indira nor her husband, Feroze Gandhi, was related to Mahatma Gandhi, the foremost political and spiritual leader in India in the twentieth century. She was, furthermore, the daughter of Jawaharlal Nehru, a follower of Mahatma Gandhi and himself a world-respected statesman. Nehru became India's first prime minister in 1947.

Gandhi was born in central India in 1917. She attended Santiniketan University before going to Oxford University in England. In 1942, she married Feroze Gandhi and had two sons, Rajiv and Sanjay. She suffered the death of her husband, Feroze and one of her sons before she herself was killed. Her husband died in 1960, and her son Sanjay was killed in an airplane crash in 1980. Both Kennedy and Ghandi suffered the loss of a son in their lifetimes, and both experienced the loss of loved ones in airplane crashes. The Kennedy family lost two members in crashes, Joseph Jr. and Kathleen, in the 1940s. Loss and death visited both the Ghandi and Kennedy families.

The lecturer provided some biographical information about Gandhi. What was it? Take a minute to see whether you wrote down the following information:

- *neither she nor her husband was related to Mahatma Gandhi*
- *the daughter of Nehru, who become prime minister in 1947*
- *born in central India in 1917*
- *attended universities in India and in England*
- *married in 1941 and had 2 sons. Her husband died in 1960, her son in 1980 in a plane crash*
- *the Kennedys and Gandhis lost sons and family members in plane crashes*

Anything else? Let's return to listening and taking notes. You will be taking notes on a longer segments of the lecture than the previous ones. Are you ready?

Gandhi began her political career as an adviser to her father Nehru. Later she herself was elected to Parliament in 1964. That same year she became Minister of Information and Broadcasting until she was chosen prime minister in 1966. She held the office of Minister of Information and Broadcasting for eleven years. In 1975, she was found guilty of illegal practices during the parliamentary election campaign of 1971. In spite of pressure to resign her Ministry office, she refused to do so. Instead of resigning, she declared a national emergency and had a number of her major opponents arrested. This turned out to be one of the biggest mistakes of her political career. Later that same year, her conviction was overturned by India's Supreme Court. Despite the fact that her conviction was overturned, when parliamentary elections were held in 1977, Indira Gandhi's Congress Party was defeated. With the defeat of the Congress Party, she lost both her position as prime minister and her seat in the Parliament. Actually, she was defeated by the party that, Morarji Desai, one of her long-time enemies, had formed just hours after he was released from prison. (Gandhi had sent him to prison.) This setback—this loss of her seat in Parliament—prompted her to organize a new "Congress-I" Party. The I, of course, stood for "Indira." In 1980, her new party gained control of Parliament and she once again became prime minister. She held the post of prime minister until her death four years later in 1984.

Throughout both her first and second terms as prime minister, she continued to lose popularity and the support of a large section of her own Congress Party. What were some of the reasons?

Remember, Gandhi was a Brahmin, a Hindu of the highest caste in India; she was privileged, aristocratic, and willful. She had a lonely childhood, a situation not unusual for a daughter of a famous and busy father, and she learned to rely heavily on herself, often giving the impression that because of her aristocratic heritage, she felt that she could do no wrong. She often demonstrated that she believed she could do no wrong when dealing with political issues and conflict situations in one of the most complex countries in the world. When Gandhi took office, for example, there was widespread unrest throughout the country because of food shortages, gross unemployment, the country's involvement in a disastrous civil war with Pakistan, and other problems too numerous to mention. At the same time, along with the United States and the former Soviet Union, India was becoming a player in the world atomic chess game by testing its first atomic bomb. India's testing of the atomic bomb caused worldwide concern—to put it mildly.

Gandhi experienced political setback, and had major personal and political troubles during her term as prime minister. But what were the major strengths of this woman who rose to the heights of power in India? Throughout her long and inconsistent political career, she worked ceaselessly to build up India's stature and place among the powerful nations of the world. She struggled to enlarge and expand India's autonomy in the areas of politics, economics, science, technology and culture. Most likely, her greatest service to India was to preserve its unity as a nation. And that she did. Today, some of her biographers fear that this contribution is being completely forgotten or downplayed.

This was one of the longest notetaking experiences you've had, thus far. How did you do? Are you beginning to figure out how you can write down a few key words, phrases, and numbers that will spark your memory when you reread them? What are those words, phrases, and numbers or statistics? (Pause.) I'll list some of these key elements. Check your notes.

- *father's adviser*
- *in 1964 elected to Parliament*
- *became Minister of Information and Broadcasting, 1964, for 11 years (Did you abbreviate the title?)*
- *chosen prime minister in 1966*

In 1975 what happened? (Pause.) How was this event connected to another event that happened in 1971? (Pause.) What was Indira's reaction to the pressure put on her to resign her Ministry office? (Pause.) The Supreme Court did something. What was it that they did? (Pause.) Let me take away your assistance or "prop," and ask you to examine your notes to see if you can reconstruct the rest of the information you heard in this segment of the lecture. Stop the tape, or take some time out, and review your notes on the section of the lecture that no prompts have been provided for. When you've finished, turn the tape on and resume the lecture.

Gandhi's murder was undoubtedly the result of great friction between India's Sikh religious group and the ruling government. Her murder prompted numerous acts of violence against the Sikh minorities throughout the country. At the time, her assassination was often described as an act of pure and pointless vengeance. But it should be noted that from the Sikh point of view, the attack on Mrs. Gandhi was not without some provocation. Throughout the years, and especially under Mrs. Gandhi, the Sikhs had faced systematic discrimination. Despite their impressive martial tradition, they were kept out of the army even though roughly thirty percent of the officers were Sikhs. The state had taken precious water rights from Sikh farmers, and India's nationalized banks would not invest in areas where Sikhs lived. In June of 1984, according to an official report, her government ordered the Indian army to attack a group of Sikh extremists who had occupied the Sikh Golden Temple in Amaritsar in north central India. Six hundred and fifty people were killed, including government soldiers. One Sikh observer explaining the violation of the Holy Shrine said, "You cannot begin to understand our reactions unless you think in terms of the Vatican being besieged and overrun by storm troopers."

Although the speaker presented a brief section of the lecture, she made a number of points about Gandhi's murder and the religious strife that afflicted India during her leadership. The speaker noted that her murder is thought to be the result of the friction between the Sikh religious groups and the ruling government. She then provided some examples of this friction and some of the consequences for both parties in the friction. Were you able to take down critical elements of the information in this section of the lecture? The examples given about the friction between the Sikhs and the government involved general events and an event that occurred in 1984. Using your notes, can you reconstruct the events in your own words? If you can, you're developing skill in listening and taking notes on some very advanced-level lectures in English. If you couldn't, just replay this segment of the lecture, and practice noting information as you listen. Let's now finish up the lecture and your notetaking exercise. Are you ready? The lecturer will draw to-gether the events that took place after the Kennedy and Gandhi assassinations.

What followed the shooting of Indira Gandhi was strangely familiar to anyone who had witnessed the Kennedy assassination in 1963. There was a struggle with the two assailants who shot the prime minister. In the struggle, one of the assailants was killed; the other was critically wounded. There was a frantic rush of the prime minister to the hospital, followed by the fruitless attempts of desperate surgeons to save the life of the political leader of the country. After the doctors failed to save the 66-year-old prime minister, her passing was announced with the simple statement: "She is no more."

Immediately after her death—in fact, the same day as her assassination—the Congress-I Party chose her son Rajiv as its head. Thus, he succeeded his mother as prime minister and served in that office until 1989. Two years later Rajiv, too, was murdered while campaigning for a parliament seat.

In total, the Gandhi family had governed India for 32 of the 37 years since its independence. The relatives of John and Robert Kennedy are also still involved in American politics, more than 30 years after John Kennedy became president of the United States. The difficulty of governing millions of people fairly and democratically, whether in the United States or India, is becoming increasingly evident as countries in the world become more and more complex in terms of their social, political, economic, and religious diversity.

How did you do with the final part of the lecture? Are you developing your confidence in your ability to listen and take notes in English? Practice will help you develop your own strategy for doing this task. It takes time and effort—and practice.

UNIT 3
Ecology and the Environment:
Natural and Human Disasters

LECTURE 5
THE DUST BOWL: NATURE AGAINST HUMANKIND

ORIENTATION LISTENING SCRIPT

One of the more tragic aspects of the Depression years of the 1920s in the United States was the weather. It seemed as if the weather was working directly against people. Floods and windstorms battered the northern and eastern sections of the country. At one time or another in the 1930s, most of the major rivers in the East rose over their banks and flooded the streets of eastern cities and towns. In fact, one flood, the Ohio River Flood of 1937, was one of the worst in the nation's history. It destroyed the homes of a half-million people. All in all, floods and windstorms in the 1930s took the lives of 3,678 people in the eastern part of the United States alone.

The weather was a major problem, not just in the north and in the east. During the '30s, throughout the entire United States, winters were unusually cold, and summers were unusually hot. In the summer of 1936, the farm state of Kansas had almost 60 days straight of 100-degree-Fahrenheit heat. That's 37.7 degrees Celsius. On July 24, 1936, the temperature reached 120 degrees Fahrenheit. That's 49 degrees on the Celsius scale. All throughout the western states, crops burned up and people were miserable. One of the worst problems of the time for the western United States was the combination of heat, drought, and the strong, hot, dusty winds which were known as "black blizzards." People and animals suffered unbearably from the heat and the black blizzards. Farm crops were ruined by the drought.

Let's back up for a moment and take a look at what had been going on in the Great Plains area before the drought, heat, and blizzards hit. For years conservationists had warned that an ecological catastrophe was coming over the Great Plains of the United States. Nature had fooled us, they said, and we had overworked the land. They noted that, generally, the Great Plains area received about 20 inches or 51 centimeters of rain each year. This was the expected amount of annual rainfall. Because of this meager—this small—amount of yearly rainfall, 100 counties in the states of Colorado, Kansas, New Mexico, Texas, and Oklahoma had been called the "Dust Bowl," even in the 1920s. But, strangely, just before the Depression years of the 1930s, the Great Plains region had received extraordinarily heavy rains. This increase in the amount of precipitation increased farming in the Plains area. Many new small farms were established. Not only that, but many of the new farmers allowed their cattle to overgraze the land, and they themselves overplowed the land. As a result, the cover vegetation of the land was severely damaged, and the topsoil was left exposed in many cases. In 1934, government conservationists estimated that 35 million acres of arable land had been completely destroyed because of overgrazing and overplowing; that's 14,164,000 hectares completely destroyed by poor farming practices. It was also estimated that another 100 million acres or 40,469,000 hectares of arable land were doomed by this misuse—this abuse of the land.

Then came a severe drought over the Plains area. The rains stopped coming. The amount of precipitation fell drastically. All of a sudden, in the early 1930s, the Dust Bowl grew from 100 counties in five states in the 1920s to 756 counties in 19 states in the '30s. Like Ireland in the 1800s, the Great Plains area of the U.S. was threatened with famine, and its people with starvation.

Along with the drought and the heat came the dust storms, or what were called "black blizzards." The first of the blizzards struck in November, 1933, in the state of South Dakota. The farm soil began blowing away in the morning. It was reported that, by noon, the sky was blacker than night. When the sun finally reappeared, farm fields had been replaced by sand. Roads, trees, fences, and farm machinery had disappeared under great hills or dunes of sand. Winds blowing over the dry, bare fields piled sand as high as 30 feet—or nine meters. Some of the clouds of dust from the storms were five miles high. Imagine. Dust clouds eight kilometers high!

The second storm struck the state of Texas. Again, farms were changed into shifting Sahara Deserts. Farmers' wives packed every windowsill, door frame, and keyhole with oiled cloth to keep out the dust and the sand, but it still penetrated and lay in piles on the floors. During another of the black blizzards in the state of Oklahoma, street lights had to be kept on day and night for three weeks straight. Oklahomans had to wear dust masks when they went outside the house, and to add to their misery, the temperature stayed at 108 degrees Fahrenheit, or if you prefer, 42.2 degrees Celsius.

Because of this deadly combination of heat, drought, and black blizzards, many of the Great Plains farmers were ruined—especially the small farmers. The "For Sale" signs in front of their small farms marked the start of the Dust Bowl migrations. Counties in the Dust Bowl area lost 60 percent of their population because of migration. In one Texas county alone, the population dropped from 40,000 to 1,000 people. Among the most unfortunate of all the migrants who were forced to abandon their farms were the Oklahoma farmers. They were called "Okies." Their misfortune and hardships were written about by the famous American novelist, John Steinbeck, in his book, *The Grapes of Wrath*. In 1940, an American movie of the same name portrayed the misery these poor Dust Bowl farmers suffered. You see, when their farms were ruined, many of the Okies moved to California, which they thought would be the "Promised Land." They hoped to find work and a better way of life in California. But what they actually found when they reached their "Promised Land" was just more drudgery, more hardship, and incredible poverty.

It's important to point out that not just the Okies suffered severe economic hardship during the years of the Depression. Many, many Americans from all areas of the country suffered. Yes, the years of the Depression were some of the most difficult the United States has ever experienced. They were years that saw both natural and economic disaster strike the country.

LISTENING AND NOTETAKING SCRIPT

One of the more tragic aspects of the Depression years of the 1920s in the United States was the weather. It seemed as if the weather was working directly against people. Floods and windstorms battered the northern and eastern sections of the country. At one time or another in the 1930s, most of the major rivers in the east rose over their banks and flooded the streets of eastern cities and towns. In fact, one flood, the Ohio River Flood of 1937, was one of the worst in the nation's history. It destroyed the homes of a half-million people. All in all, floods and windstorms in the 1930s took the lives of 3,678 people in the eastern part of the United States alone.

The weather was a major problem, not just in the north and in the east. During the '30s, throughout the entire United States, winters were unusually cold, and summers were unusually hot. In the summer of 1936, the farm state of Kansas had almost 60 days straight of 100-degree-Fahrenheit heat. That's 37.7 degrees Celsius. On July 24, 1936, the temperature reached 120 degrees Fahrenheit. That's 49 degrees on the Celsius scale. All throughout the western states, crops burned up and people were miserable. One of the worst problems of the time for the western United States was the combination of heat, drought, and the strong, hot, dusty winds which were known as "black blizzards." People and animals suffered unbearably from the heat and the black blizzards. Farm crops were ruined by the drought.

How are you doing with your notetaking? At the start of the lecture, you heard the lecturer say that "one of the more tragic aspects of the Depression years of the 1920s in the United States was the weather. It seemed as if the weather was working directly against people." What did he say next? Right. He gave some specific examples of the weather's working against people. What were the examples? Did you write down the examples in your notes? There wasn't much time to write down all the examples, now, was there? How did (or could) you handle the constraint of time? You could have noted just one example during the lecture, and then after class, you could plan to meet with a classmate who also took notes and you could compare and flesh out your notes with his or her help. For example, perhaps during the lecture, you only had time to write down in your notes the phrase "half a million people," but perhaps you didn't have time to note that the homes of these half a million people were destroyed by the Ohio River Flood of 1937. When you have time, be sure to fill in any of the information you missed during class. Don't, in other words, be discouraged if you cannot take down the information verbatim, or word for word. Just work on developing the ability to listen and synthesize information in note form which you can make fuller at a later time.

But let's return to assessing how successful you were in taking notes on the information you just heard. The lecturer talked about the Ohio Flood of 1937. He mentioned that floods and windstorms in the 1930s killed more than 3,000 people in the eastern U.S. What was the exact number he mentioned? Check your notes. It was 3,678. The lecturer also pointed out that the weather was a problem in the entire U.S. Why? Can you look at your notes to find the answers to that question? What happened in the summer of 1936? What was the temperature on July 24, 1936? Did you get down both the Celsius and Fahrenheit temperatures? Writing down both numbers would certainly be difficult to do, but I hope you managed to note either the Celsius or the Fahrenheit number. You could figure out which was Celsius and which was Fahrenheit because of the magnitude of the numbers, couldn't you? What was the worst problem for the western part of the United States? How did you write the phrase "black blizzards"? Did you just write down two "b"s? Or did you do something else? Well, as long as you could go back to your notes and interpret the symbol, the abbreviation, or the idiosyncratic notation—the individualistic notation—you wrote down, you're doing ok.

Let's return to the lecture. Think for a moment about the general topic that will be discussed in this segment of the lecture—the ecological catastrophe that hit the Great Plains. The speaker will talk about the unusual amount of rainfall and the destruction of the farmland by animal overgrazing and farmer overplowing. This will lead him into the discussion of the Great Drought. (Pause.) But we will take a break from listening and notetaking at that point. Are you ready?

Let's back up for a moment and take a look at what had been going on in the Great Plains area before the drought, heat, and blizzards hit. For years conservationists had warned that an ecological catastrophe was coming over the Great Plains of the United States. Nature had fooled us, they said, and we had overworked the land. They noted that, generally, the Great

Plains area received about 20 inches or 51 centimeters of rain each year. This was the expected amount of annual rainfall. Because of this meager—this small—amount of yearly rainfall, 100 counties in the states of Colorado, Kansas, New Mexico, Texas, and Oklahoma had been called the "Dust Bowl," even in the 1920s. But, strangely, just before the Depression years of the 1930s, the Great Plains region had received extraordinarily heavy rains. This increase in the amount of precipitation increased farming in the Plains area. Many new small farms were established. Not only that, but many of the new farmers allowed their cattle to overgraze the land, and they themselves overplowed the land. As a result, the cover vegetation of the land was severely damaged, and the topsoil was left exposed in many cases. In 1934, government conservationists estimated that 35 million acres of arable land had been completely destroyed because of overgrazing and overplowing; that's 14,164,000 hectares completely destroyed by poor farming practices. It was also estimated that another 100 million acres or 40,469,000 hectares of arable land were doomed by this misuse—this abuse of the land.

Then came a severe drought over the Plains area. The rains stopped coming. The amount of precipitation fell drastically. All of a sudden, in the early 1930s, the Dust Bowl grew from 100 counties in five states in the 1920s to 756 counties in 19 states in the '30s. Like Ireland in the 1800s, the Great Plains area of the U.S. was threatened with famine, and its people with starvation.

This part of the lecture was rather brief, but in this segment the lecturer provided a good deal of information about the historical background of the ecological catastrophe and the reasons for drought, heat, and blizzards. The speaker begins by noting that before the catastrophe, nature had played a trick on the people who lived in the Great Plains states. What kind of trick? Well, there was much more rain than usual. What did he say about how much rain the Great Plains area usually received in one year? Can you locate that piece of information in your notes? (Pause.) Good. Do you know how many counties in Colorado, Kansas, New Mexico, Texas, and Oklahoma had been called the "Dust Bowl" even in the 1920s? Check your notes. Did you abbreviate all the names of the states? Good. Well, when the Plains states received heavier amounts of rainfall, what did the farmers do? Do you need to look at your notes or can you remember this particular bit of information? You can probably remember it now, but if you had to recall the information a few weeks after you heard the lecture, I'm sure you would be happy that you wrote the abbreviations down in your notes. The notes would help you reconstruct the information you heard at an earlier time. Ok. Well, what happened when the farmers allowed their cattle to overgraze the land and when they themselves overplowed the land? Check your notes. Do you have some symbol, word, or notation that indicates that the "cover vegetation" of the land was severely damaged and the "topsoil" left exposed? The lecturer gave you some statistics about the amount of arable land that was damaged and destroyed as a result of the overplowing and the overgrazing. What were those statistics? Are they in your notes? It's okay if you missed one or two of them as long as you check with a classmate after the class to make your notes as complete as possible. Did you also write down that when the rains stopped and the precipitation level fell, the Dust Bowl grew from 100 counties in five states to 756 counties in 19 states? Famine and starvation threatened the U.S. as famine and starvation threatened Ireland in the 1800s.

Let's continue with the lecture as he begins to talk about the change that came over the Great Plains when the drought and the dust storms began. There will be no interruption during this final segment of the lecture. You'll have to rely on your developing ability to take notes to synthesize the information in notes during this final part of the lecture.

Along with the drought and the heat came the dust storms, or what were called "black blizzards." The first of the blizzards struck in November, 1933, in the state of South Dakota. The farm soil began blowing away in the morning. It was reported that, by noon, the sky was blacker than night. When the sun finally reappeared, farm fields had been replaced by sand. Roads, trees, fences, and farm machinery had disappeared under great hills or dunes of sand. Winds blowing over the dry, bare fields piled sand as high as 30 feet—or nine meters. Some of the clouds of dust from the storms were five miles high. Imagine. Dust clouds eight kilometers high!

The second storm struck the state of Texas. Again, farms were changed into shifting Sahara Deserts. Farmers' wives packed every windowsill, door frame, and keyhole with oiled cloth to keep out the dust and the sand, but it still penetrated and lay in piles on the floors. During another of the black blizzards in the state of Oklahoma, street lights had to be kept on day and night for three weeks straight. Oklahomans had to wear dust masks when they went outside the house, and to add to their misery, the temperature stayed at 108 degrees Fahrenheit, or if you prefer, 42.2 degrees Celsius.

Because of this deadly combination of heat, drought, and black blizzards, many of the Great Plains farmers were ruined—especially the small farmers. The "For Sale" signs in front of their small farms marked the start of the Dust Bowl migrations. Counties in the Dust Bowl area lost 60 percent of their population because of migration. In one Texas county alone, the population dropped from 40,000 to 1,000 people. Among the most unfortunate of all the migrants who were forced to abandon their farms were the Oklahoma farmers. They were called "Okies." Their misfortune and hardships were written about by the famous American novelist, John Steinbeck, in his book, *The Grapes of Wrath*. In 1940, an American movie of the same name portrayed the misery these poor Dust Bowl farmers suffered. You see, when their farms were ruined, many of the Okies moved to California, which they thought would be the "Promised Land." They hoped to find work and a better way of life in California. But what they actually found when they reached their "Promised Land" was just more drudgery, more hardship, and incredible poverty.

It's important to point out that not just the Okies suffered severe economic hardship during the years of the Depression. Many, many Americans from all areas of the country suffered. Yes, the years of the Depression were some of the most difficult the United States has ever experienced. They were years that saw both natural and economic disaster strike the country.

Well, how did you do? Are you beginning to feel that you're increasing your ability to listen to information presented in English and to synthesize the information in a form that will allow you to reconstruct the information at a later date? I hope so. If you feel as though you need to listen to this lecture again, do so. To develop a skill, you must practice—and practice—and practice.

ORIENTATION LISTENING SCRIPT

The dust storms that hit the midwestern part of the United States in the 1930s caused ecological and economic disaster for the farmers living in the region. As you heard in the lecture on the Dust Bowl, the disaster had economic and political consequences not only for the Dust Bowl farmers, but also for all Americans. Well, nature turned against those living in the Midwest again 60 years later. The Great Flood of '93 that struck the western Plains states of the United States turned out to be an all-time monster. It might, in fact, go down as the worst flood in U.S. history, and its devastation has caused extreme misery for many farmers and their families.

Let me illustrate the magnitude of the flood by telling you something about the Mississippi River. First, let me explain what the word "Mississippi" means. Mississippi is an Indian, or Native American, name meaning "Big River." The river is also called the "Big Muddy" because it carries so much dirt and mud along as it travels. It is referred to by many as the "Father of Rivers."

The Mississippi is the most important river in the United States. It is located just to the east of the area that made up the Dust Bowl in the 1930s, and it forms the boundary of 10 of the 50 states in the U.S. The Mississippi is 2,348 miles long. If the Missouri River, which flows into the Mississippi, is considered to be part of the Mississippi, the combined river would be 3,680 miles long. That would make it the second longest river in the world. (The Nile River, which is 4,000 miles long, is the longest river in the world.) The Mississippi has played a vital role in the economic development of the United States, particularly during the last half of the nineteenth and the early half of the twentieth centuries. At this time the river was a major boon to the growth of industry. The river provided a convenient way to transport goods and materials to and from many important industrial cities such as Chicago. Water-powered electricity is another benefit that encouraged the growth of industry on the banks of the Mississippi. There are 29 dams on the river providing power for factories and businesses. Industrial cities located along its bank include Minneapolis, Minnesota; St. Louis, Missouri; and New Orleans, Louisiana. The famous American author, Mark Twain, wrote many stories about the Mississippi as it was a hundred years ago. After railroads were built in the western parts of the U.S., the Mississippi became less important than it was in the 1800s, but it has continued to be the most important waterway in the United States.

Most of the year, the Mississippi is a beautiful, peaceful, and functional river, but in 1993 it proved a threat to the people, businesses, and farms lining the "Father of Rivers." Let me describe the watery natural disaster that took such a toll in the summer of 1993.

What caused the Great Flood of 1993? And how did it affect the many people living in the Midwest? For five weeks in the early summer of 1993, a high pressure system over the eastern part of the United States had been pumping warm moist air from the Gulf of Mexico and dumping it into thunderstorms. These thunderstorms, in turn, dumped water into the river and the states around it quickly and for days at a time. An extreme example of how much rain fell is Papillion, Nebraska, which received an inch of rain in only six minutes. All of this rain has to go somewhere, and since the river is at the lowest point in the midwestern U.S., all of the water flows into the Mississippi. As a result, the amount of water increased dramatically to the point that the banks of the river could not hold all the water in.

Towns were flooded. Some residents of these towns had to travel around town in boats rather than cars. Many homes were under water and home furnishings were destroyed or carried away by the slowly moving flood waters. Many people had to evacuate and move into the homes of friends or relatives or live in refugee shelters. As for the farmers in the path of the "Father of Rivers," their crops were lost, in most cases for the whole year. And why was that? Well, the Mississippi generally floods in the spring, which gives the farmers a chance to replant and harvest a reduced crop. This time, however, the flood began in July and the farmers weren't able to replant in August when the flood waters went down.

However, unlike the small farmers who experienced the Dust Bowl disaster in the 1930s, many of the midwestern farmers will survive the 1990s disaster. There are several reasons for this. First of all, although many people involved in the flood did not have flood insurance, many others did. Government and charitable organizations will also help these people pull through the disaster. The federal government promised the people in the flooded states 2.5 billion dollars in flood relief assistance. The Federal Emergency Management Agency moved with speed to assist the people in the area with food, drinking water, evacuation centers, and other needs. All of this will help ease the pain of the disaster for the people living on the banks of the Mississippi, but all of this will not completely erase the damage. Some calculated that the estimated damage to the area is around 8 billion dollars. That doesn't even count the time people spent cleaning debris, sewage, and layers of mud from their houses and belongings. You probably remember how much people complained of the dust in the Dust Bowl. Well, after the Great Flood of '93, people had to deal with lots and lots of mud that the "Big Muddy" deposited during the flooding.

There is no doubt that the people on the banks of the Mississippi went through a lot of pain and suffering during and after the flood, but the damage was not as severe as it was in the Dust Bowl. Most of these farmers will not have to leave their farms to travel in search of a new life. They may be more concerned about living and farming in the flood plain, but this land is some of the most fertile and scenic land in the United States. Ironically, it is fertile and scenic because of the very river that made it so dangerous in 1993. So, people will probably continue to build and farm here; but, after the Great Flood of '93, they will never forget that they are subject to the whims of Mother Nature when it comes to their farms and livelihood.

LISTENING AND NOTETAKING SCRIPT

As you listen to the lecture this time, I'd like to ask you not only to outline the information you hear but also to fill in the outline as you listen. When you heard the lecture for the first time, you were looking at an outline that presented the overall structure of the lecture. So, in addition to writing down abbreviations of individual words, phrases, symbols, and so forth, try to create both an outline and a recording of general and detailed information. Are you ready?

The dust storms that hit the midwestern part of the United States in the 1930s caused ecological and economic disaster for the farmers living in the region. As you heard in the lecture on the Dust Bowl, the disaster had economic and political consequences not only for the Dust Bowl farmers, but also for all Americans. Well, nature turned against those living in the Midwest again 60 years later. The Great Flood of '93 that struck the western Plains states of the United States turned out to be an all-time monster. It might, in fact, go down as the worst flood in U.S. history, and its devastation has caused extreme misery for many farmers and their families.

Let me illustrate the magnitude of the flood by telling you something about the Mississippi River. First, let me explain what the word "Mississippi" means. Mississippi is an Indian, or Native American, name meaning "Big River." The river is also called the "Big Muddy" because it carries so much dirt and mud along as it travels. It is referred to by many as the "Father of Rivers."

Ok. How are you doing? Were you able to write down the outline of this section of the lecture? What were the main elements of the outline? Recall the orientation listening outline. It contained the following information about the Great Flood of '93:

- *It caused misery in the Midwest (or as the lecturer said, "In the western Plains states of the United States).*
- *It occurred 60 years after the Dust Bowl.*
- *It may have been the worst flood in U.S. history.*
- *It caused devastation for the farmers and their families.*

You didn't have to take down every word or phrase. Did you get the main points mentioned in your outline? Fine. Let's continue. The next segment is longer than the one you just heard. Are you ready?

The Mississippi is the most important river in the United States. It is located just to the east of the area that made up the Dust Bowl in the 1930s, and it forms the boundary of 10 of the 50 states in the U.S. The Mississippi is 2,348 miles long. If the Missouri River, which flows into the Mississippi, is considered to be part of the Mississippi, the combined river would be 3,680 miles long. That would make it the second longest river in the world. (The Nile River, which is 4,000 miles long, is the longest river in the world.) The Mississippi has played a vital role in the economic development of the United States, particularly during the last half of the nineteenth and the early half of the twentieth centuries. At this time the river was a major boon to the growth of industry. The river provided a convenient way to transport goods and materials to and from many important industrial cities such as Chicago. Water-powered electricity is another benefit that encouraged the growth of industry on the banks of the Mississippi. There are 29 dams on the river providing power for factories and businesses. Industrial cities located along its bank include Minneapolis, Minnesota; St. Louis, Missouri; and New Orleans, Louisiana. The famous American author, Mark Twain, wrote many stories about the Mississippi as it was a hundred years ago. After railroads were built in the western parts of the U.S., the Mississippi became less important than it was in the 1800s, but it has continued to be the most important waterway in the United States.

Most of the year, the Mississippi is a beautiful, peaceful, and functional river, but in 1993 it proved a threat to the people, businesses, and farms lining the "Father of Rivers." Let me describe the watery natural disaster that took such a toll in the summer of 1993.

What caused the Great Flood of 1993? And how did it affect the many people living in the Midwest? For five weeks in the early summer of 1993, a high pressure system over the eastern part of the United States had been pumping warm moist air from the Gulf of Mexico and dumping it into thunderstorms. These thunderstorms, in turn, dumped water into the river and the states around it quickly and for days at a time. An extreme example of how much rain fell is Papillion, Nebraska, which received an inch of rain in only six minutes. All of this rain has to go somewhere, and since the river is at the lowest point in the midwestern U.S., all of the water flows into the Mississippi. And as a result, the amount of water increased dramatically to the point that the banks of the river could not hold all the water in.

Towns were flooded. Some residents of these towns had to travel around town in boats rather than cars. Many homes were under water and home furnishings were destroyed or carried away by the slowly moving flood waters. Many people had to evacuate and move into the homes of friends or relatives or live in refugee shelters. As for the farmers in the path of the "Father of Rivers," their crops were lost, in most cases for the whole year. And why was that? Well, the Mississippi generally floods in the spring, which gives the farmers a chance to replant and harvest a reduced crop. This time, however, the flood began in July and the farmers weren't able to replant in August when the flood waters went down.

Let's pause for a minute so you can check your notes. I'll review the outline presented during the orientation listening, and you check your notes. Make any changes or additions that you wish to while I reiterate the major pieces of information given by the lecturer.

She started off by saying that most of the year, the Mississippi is a beautiful, peaceful, and functional river. She called it the "Father of Rivers," in fact. She then talked about its size . . . its length, that is. How long is the Mississippi River itself? (Pause.) How long is it if the Missouri River is included in its size? (Pause.) Fine. What was the final statistic of this type that the lecturer mentioned? Why did she reference the Nile, do you think? (Pause.) The lecturer did not say why she talked about the Nile, but it should be obvious that she was trying to show that the Missouri-Mississippi Rivers are enormously large . . . Or should I say "long."

What did the speaker mention next? (Pause.) Right, she spoke about the importance of the river to the economic development of the U.S.—particularly to the country's development in the latter part of the 19th century. What examples did she use to back up this point? Can you search your notes and answer that question? (Pause.) Finally, the lecturer made mention of an important American writer. Who was that?

Well, how are you doing? Did you continue taking down the information you could while listening? Let's check. The speaker started to talk about the Great Flood of 1993. An outline of the points made would include the following phrases:

- *large amounts of rain fell*
- *towns were flooded*
- *people traveled by boats through their towns*
- *homes were evacuated*
- *furnishings were destroyed*
- *crops were lost for the year*

Why? Right. The farmers weren't able to replant because the river flooded so late in the year.

Ok. Let's finish listening to the lecture. This next segment is much shorter, so relax a bit and take your notes in outline form, with any additional notations you wish to make. She begins drawing a parallel with the farmers who suffered so badly during the Dust Bowl catastrophe—as the speaker says, "the Dust Bowl disaster." Are you ready?

However, unlike the small farmers who experienced the Dust Bowl disaster in the 1930s, many of the midwestern farmers will survive the 1990s disaster. There are several reasons for this. First of all, although many people involved in the flood did not have flood insurance, many others did. Government and charitable organizations will also help these people pull through the disaster. The federal government promised the people in the flooded states 2.5 billion dollars in flood relief assistance. The Federal Emergency Management Agency moved with speed to assist the people in the area with food, drinking water, evacuation centers, and other needs. All of this will help ease the pain of the disaster for the people living on the banks of the Mississippi, but all of this will not completely erase the damage. Some calculated that the estimated damage to the area is around 8 billion dollars. That doesn't even count the time people spent cleaning debris, sewage, and layers of mud from their houses and belongings. You probably remember how much people complained of the dust in the Dust Bowl. Well, after the Great Flood of '93, people had to deal with lots and lots of mud that the "Big Muddy" deposited during the flooding.

There is no doubt that the people on the banks of the Mississippi went through a lot of pain and suffering during and after the flood, but the damage was not as severe as it was in the Dust Bowl. Most of these farmers will not have to leave their farms to travel in search of a new life. They may be more concerned about living and farming in the flood plain, but this land is some of the most fertile and scenic land in the United States. Ironically, it is fertile and scenic because of the very river that made it so dangerous in 1993. So, people will probably continue to build and farm here; but, after the

Great Flood of '93, they will never forget that they are subject to the whims of Mother Nature when it comes to their farms and livelihood.

I'd like you to refer back to the orientation listening outline of the lecture and check how different (and I hope more complete) your notes are from those in the orientation outline. You should be developing and improving your own style of notetaking in English. How are you doing?

UNIT 4
Contemporary Social Issues: Women, Men, and Changing Roles

LECTURE 7
THE WOMEN'S MOVEMENT: FROM LIBERATION TO FEMINISM

ORIENTATION LISTENING SCRIPT

The Women's Movement in the United States is a social movement that is nearly a century and a half old, according to Barbara Ryan, author of *Feminism and the Women's Movement.* According to Ryan, organized activity on behalf of women's rights began in the mid 1800s, when both by law and by custom, women were considered "nonpersons." Married women, for example, were prevented by law from inheriting property, from controlling the money they earned, or from retaining custody of their children if they were divorced by their husbands. In addition, no woman was allowed to vote on the laws that governed her life.

In the early 1900s, important changes occurred in the social and political climate in Europe and America as a result of World War I. After the war, a number of countries granted women the right to vote, and in 1920, American women gained the right to vote. Twenty years later, another war brought more major social changes that affected the lives of many men and women. One of the social changes involved women working outside the home. During World War II, large numbers of women entered the job market to do the jobs of the men who had been drafted into military service. A great many of these women became factory workers, and they proved themselves to be capable and dependable workers. Today, women have gained more employment and job opportunities, and they hold different jobs and occupations. Women are breaking into male-dominated fields from sportswriting to police work to firefighting, though their progress into these male-dominated professions is slow. In fact, women make up 1.5 percent of the 200,000 professional firefighters in the U.S. today, and they make up 4 percent of airline pilots and navigators.

In addition to entering male-dominated professions, many women are starting their own businesses today, and operating successful businesses. It is becoming more and more common to find women occupying positions of leadership in American business. In fact, women-owned business is among the fastest-growing segments of the U.S. economy. The Small Business Administration counts more than 5 million women-owned American businesses, and the Small Business Administration predicts that women will own nearly 40 percent (others say half) of all small businesses in the U.S. by the year 2000. The entry of women into leadership positions in American business is occurring rapidly. From 1980 to 1988, the number of business men and women—entrepreneurs—increased 56 percent overall, but during that period, the number of female entrepreneurs grew 82 percent. In the same time frame, entrepreneurial revenues in the United States grew 56 percent overall, but those of female entrepreneurs soared 129 percent. In 1992, women-owned businesses employed more people domestically than the Fortune 500 companies did worldwide. Why are women entrepreneurs so successful? The founder and president of the American Women's Economic Development Corporation in New York, Beatrice Fitzpatrick, says "A woman would no more let her business fail than she would let someone kill her child." But for some women, success in business has not come without the costs of overwork, burnout, and potential damage to health, friendships, or family relationships. According to the authors of the book *Megatrends for Women*, the great challenge for millions of successful women entrepreneurs and other professionals is to maintain their success while being sure that they have a balance between work and their family and social lives.

Women have advanced to leadership positions not only in business, but also in politics. Women have become important political leaders all over the world, though politics is still a largely male-dominated world. For instance, in 1969 in the U.S., only 4 percent of the state lawmakers were women. By 1993, this number had grown by 500 percent, and 20.4 percent of state legislators were women. Although this may seem like a great increase, it must be remembered that women make up more than 50 percent of the population in the U.S., so they are not yet receiving equal representation in the world of politics in the United States. The U.S. has not yet had a woman president, for example, although women have served as presidents of Ireland, Nicaragua, and the Philippines. Many other countries have had female political leaders. Women have served as prime ministers in France, Turkey, Pakistan, Canada, and Bangladesh. Margaret Thatcher became prime minister of Great Britain in 1979.

The family has changed a lot since women have become so active outside the home. Today, only 10 percent of American families have the traditional working father and the mother who stays home to take care of the children. To make up for the time that women are spending out of the home, many men are having to play a more active role in raising their children. Government and businesses are also becoming more concerned about helping working families with child care, but much more needs to be done to help women and men take care of their children while they are at work. In spite of the fact that the rate of women's participation in the work force rose from 27 percent in 1940 to 44 percent in 1985 (including more than half of all women with a child under the age of one year old), there is still no government-sponsored child care or parental leave policy in the United States. A major obstacle to women's emancipation lies in the lack of government-sponsored social service support for working women who have children to support, according to Barbara Ryan.

Because some problems are still preventing some women from taking an equal place in society, many people believe that a Women's Movement is still necessary; however, many diverse opinions have emerged about how to achieve equality for women and men in work, education, politics, and the home. Some activists in the Women's Movement call themselves feminists, while others who resist political activism choose not to label themselves "feminists" because they feel that the U.S. media often portrays feminists as people who are anti-men. Most feminists do not take such an attitude at all. In any case, the word "feminism" and the principles of feminism are not easy to define because they mean different things to different people. In her book *Feminism and the Women's Movement*, Barbara Ryan provides a number of definitions of the term "feminism." She quotes one woman who says that in her opinion "feminism represents the best of what it means to be human. Anybody can be a feminist, except you have to work at it. Basically, to me, it is the belief that everybody should have the opportunity to be the best that they can be and we ought to have a world that encourages that."

The names and terms associated with the movement, however, are not nearly as important as the changes that feminism and the Women's Movement have caused in American society. Because of this century-and-a-half old movement, women are contributing more to American society, and society is benefiting from their contributions. As a result of the Women's Movement, Women's Liberation, and feminism, women are enjoying new freedom, new opportunities, new responsibility—and new headaches.

LISTENING AND NOTETAKING SCRIPT

The Women's Movement in the United States is a social movement that is nearly a century and a half old, according to Barbara Ryan, author of *Feminism and the Women's Movement*. According to Ryan, organized activity on behalf of women's rights began in the mid 1800s when both by law and by custom, women were considered "nonpersons." Married women, for example, were prevented by law from inheriting property, from controlling the money they earned, or from retaining custody of their children if they were divorced by their husbands. In addition, no woman was allowed to vote on the laws that governed her life.

Let's stop for a minute and check your notetaking. What were the salient, or important, pieces of information you just heard? Did you write down the following facts? The Women's Movement in the U.S. is nearly 150 years old. Did you have time to write down the name of Barbara Ryan's book? Probably not. But did you attempt to abbreviate the title or to make some notation that you could return to after the lecture was finished? The title of the book is Feminism and the Women's Movement. *Did you spell Ryan's name correctly? Again, don't worry if you didn't. You could ask a friend after the lecture how her name is spelled. Actually, it's spelled R-y-a-n. Did you also write down that women were considered "nonpersons"?*

Did you note that women couldn't inherit property, control their money, or keep their children if they got divorced? Let's continue with the lecture.

In the early 1900s, important changes occurred in the social and political climate in Europe and America as a result of World War I. After the war, a number of countries granted women the right to vote, and in 1920, American women gained the right to vote. Twenty years later, another war brought more major social changes that affected the lives of many men and women. One of the social changes involved women working outside the home. During World War II, large numbers of women entered the job market to do the jobs of the men who had been drafted into military service. A great many of these women became factory workers, and they proved themselves to be capable and dependable workers. Today, women have gained more employment and job opportunities, and they hold different jobs and occupations. Women are breaking into male-dominated fields from sportswriting to police work to firefighting, though their progress into these male-dominated professions is slow. In fact, women make up 1.5 percent of the 200,000 professional firefighters in the U.S. today, and they make up 4 percent of airline pilots and navigators.

There was a good deal more information in this section of the lecture than there was in the opening section of the lecture. Did you write down:

- *that World War I brought social and political changes?*
- *that after the war, many women were granted the right to vote?*
- *that in the U.S., women got the vote in 1920?*
- *that after World War II women began working outside the home in jobs that men had done?*
- *that the women were good workers—good factory workers?*
- *that today, women are entering male-dominated fields, for example, sportswriting, police work, and firefighting?*

How much of this information were you able to write down? Let's continue practicing. Listen and write what you think is important, and be sure not to try to write each word or even each sentence.

In addition to entering male-dominated professions, many women are starting their own businesses today, and operating successful businesses. It is becoming more and more common to find women occupying positions of leadership in American business. In fact, women-owned business is among the fastest-growing segments of the U.S. economy. The Small Business Administration counts more than 5 million women-owned American businesses, and the Small Business Administration predicts that women will own nearly 40 percent (others say half) of all small businesses in the U.S. by the year 2000. The entry of women into leadership positions in American business is occurring rapidly. From 1980 to 1988, the number of business men and women—entrepreneurs—increased 56 percent overall, but during that period, the number of female entrepreneurs grew 82 percent. In the same time frame, entrepreneurial revenues in the United States grew 56 percent overall, but those of female entrepreneurs soared 129 percent. In 1992, women-owned businesses employed more people domestically than the Fortune 500 companies did worldwide. Why are women entrepreneurs so successful? The founder and president of the American Women's Economic Development Corporation in New York, Beatrice Fitzpatrick, says "A woman would no more let her business fail than she would let someone kill her child." But for some women, success in business has not come without the costs of overwork, burnout, and potential damage to health, friendships, or family relationships. According to the authors of the book *Megatrends for Women*, the great challenge for millions of successful women entrepreneurs and other professionals is to maintain their success while being sure that they have a balance between work and their family and social lives.

Now what did you do with all the information in that segment of the lecture? Perhaps you just noted key words throughout? The information was dense, and it's unlikely you could write down more than a skeleton outline of the information. The important thing is that what you wrote is enough to help you reconstruct the key information when you review your notes. Let me reiterate the information in skeleton form and you check your notes. I repeat that you didn't need to write down all the information. You needed to write enough codes that you could reconstruct the information when reading over your note codes.

Ok. The lecturer mentioned the following pieces of information: Women are becoming successful in business and taking on leadership positions in businesses. Women-owned business is fast-growing. There are more than 5 million women-owned businesses in America, according to a report from the Small Business Administration. In fact, women-owned businesses employed more people domestically than the Fortune 500 companies did worldwide. Success in business has cost women dearly. They have experienced overwork, burnout, health problems, and success has been hard on friendships and family relationships. The authors of Megatrends for Women *say women face the challenge of maintaining success while keeping a balance between work and their family and social lives. Ok. Let's return to the lecture.*

Women have advanced to leadership positions not only in business, but also in politics. Women have become important political leaders all over the world, though politics is still a largely male-dominated world. For instance, in 1969 in the U.S., only 4 percent of the state lawmakers were women. By 1993, this number had grown by 500 percent, and 20.4 percent of state legislators were women. Although this may seem like a great increase, it must be remembered that women make up more than 50 percent of the population in the U.S., so they are not yet receiving equal representation in the world of politics in the United States. The U.S. has not yet had a woman president, for example, although women have served as presidents of Ireland, Nicaragua, and the Philippines. Many other countries have had female political leaders. Women have served as prime ministers in France, Turkey, Pakistan, Canada, and Bangladesh. Margaret Thatcher became prime minister of Great Britain in 1979.

The lecturer mentioned some of the important women political leaders—although there aren't many of them, are there? She mentioned that a small number of the state lawmakers in the U.S. are women. What was that percentage? Can you answer this question by looking at your notes? If so, great. There were a number of other statistics in this segment of the lecture.

What was said about 500%? What about 20.4%? Did you write down a statistic of more than 50%? Did you remember to write 50% plus, not just 50%? What did the lecturer say about this statistic? Can you name the countries which have had women prime ministers? Look at your notes to find this information. Did you abbreviate the names of the countries? "Fr" for France? "Tur" for Turkey? And so forth. Fine. Let's continue with the lecture with the discussion of how the family has changed since women started working outside the home.

The family has changed a lot since women have become so active outside the home. Today, only 10 percent of American families have the traditional working father and the mother who stays home to take care of the children. To make up for the time that women are spending out of the home, many men are having to play a more active role in raising their children. Government and businesses are also becoming more concerned about helping working families with child care, but much more needs to be done to help women and men take care of their children while they are at work. In spite of the fact that the rate of women's participation in the work force rose from 27 percent in 1940 to 44 percent in 1985 (including more than half of all women with a child under the age of one year old), there is still no government-sponsored child care or parental leave policy in the United States. A major obstacle to women's emancipation lies in the lack of government-sponsored social service support for working women who have children to support, according to Barbara Ryan.

Once again, the lecturer provided a number of statistics to support her statement that the traditional family has undergone change. She mentioned that fathers are taking a more active role in raising their children. She also said that government and business are becoming concerned about helping families with child care, but they haven't done enough. Many more women are working. In 1940, what percentage of women were working? Can you find that information in your notes? (Pause.) Yes, 27%. What did that percentage change to in 1985? (Pause.) Right, 44%. That's quite a change! Ok. Although so many women are working today, there still is no government-sponsored child care or parental leave policy in the U.S., if you can believe it! The lecturer noted that Barbara Ryan, the author of the book mentioned at the beginning of the lecture, suggests that this lack of a government-sponsored social service support for working women is a major obstacle to women's liberation, or as she said, "women's emancipation."

Let's return to the lecture now as the speaker finished up her talk. You will take notes on this segment without any prompting. See how you do on your own.

Because some problems are still preventing some women from taking an equal place in society, many people believe that a Women's Movement is still necessary; however, many diverse opinions have emerged about how to achieve equality for women and men in work, education, politics, and the home. Some activists in the Women's Movement call themselves feminists, while others who resist political activism choose not to label themselves "feminists" because they feel that the U.S. media often portrays feminists as people who are anti-men. Most feminists do not take such an attitude at all. In any case, the word "feminism" and the principles of feminism are not easy to define because they mean different things to different people. In her book *Feminism and the Women's Movement,* Barbara Ryan provides a number of definitions of the term "feminism." She quotes one woman who says that in her opinion "feminism represents the best of what it means to be human. Anybody can be a feminist, except you have to work at it. Basically, to me, it is the belief that everybody should have the opportunity to be the best that they can be and we ought to have a world that encourages that."

The names and terms associated with the movement, however, are not nearly as important as the changes that feminism and the Women's Movement have caused in American society. Because of this century-and-a-half old movement, women are contributing more to American society, and society is benefiting from their contributions. As a result of the Women's Movement, Women's Liberation and feminism, women are enjoying new freedom, new opportunities, new responsibility—and new headaches.

Well, your task is now complete. Are you beginning to feel more comfortable with listening and taking down notes that can be used to spark your memory and to reconstruct the information you heard? You will be developing your own strategies for taking effective notes as we continue to work through the Advanced Listening Comprehension *notetaking program.*

LECTURE 8
THE MEN'S MOVEMENT: WHAT DOES IT MEAN TO BE A MAN?

ORIENTATION LISTENING SCRIPT

The Women's Movement has gained a lot of attention in recent years in North America and in countries around the world, as you heard in the last lecture. The Women's Movement has inspired many women to fight for equal rights and treatment in their homes, their personal relationships, and at work. It has also forced many women to examine and to rethink the roles they play in society. However, not only have women begun to examine and rethink the roles they play at home, at work, and in modern society as a whole, but men also have begun to examine and rethink the roles they play in society, and to examine and rethink the various and changing roles they must play at home and work today.

Men have also begun to react in both positive and negative ways to the new expectations they must meet at home and at work. Some men are adjusting well to the new roles they must play as more and more women enter the job market, and some men are pleased that their wives and partners have jobs outside the home. However, some of the role changes men are having to make to accommodate their working wives and girlfriends, as well as some of the new expectations concerning their masculinity, are causing some of them a good deal of stress, anger, and confusion. Some are even asking the question "What does it mean to be a real man in today's world?" Many are confused about how they should treat women, whether these women are their female colleagues at work, their friends, or their wives. Some feel they are no longer "king of the castle" at home. As a result of this confusion and unhappiness, a countermovement called the Men's Movement has sprung up alongside the Women's Movement in the United

States. Men in the movement seek to provide one another with the support they need to cope with the stresses and strains of being a man in today's world, and to cope with the stresses and strains brought about by the professional advances made and the personal freedoms won by women in many countries over the past few decades.

Some women view the Men's Movement as a backlash against the professional advances they have made and personal freedoms they have won as a result of the Women's Movement. Many men (and many women, also) see the Men's Movement as men's need to form a brotherhood for psychological support, just as women have formed support groups with other women. Others see the Men's Movement as men's attempt and need to understand more fully what it means and takes to be a "real man" at the close of the 20th century, when traditional definitions of manhood are changing or are under attack in many countries around the world.

To begin this discussion of some of the catalysts for the Men's Movement, I'll say a few words about why some women consider the Men's Movement a reaction against the Women's Movement—what the well-known author Susan Faludi calls the "backlash" against the Women's Movement. Ms. Faludi suggests that some men feel that women are becoming too independent and powerful today as a result of the professional advances they have made in the workplace and because of the personal reedoms they have gained in their family and personal relationships. She notes that the resentment of some men toward women's gaining power is not a recent phenomenon. More than 1,900 years ago, the women of Rome tried to repeal a law that forbade them from riding in horse-drawn chariots and from wearing multicolored dresses. In 195 B.C., the Roman senator Cato expressed the fear that the women of Rome had become so powerful that the independence of the men of Rome had been lost in their homes, and was being trampled underfoot in public. In her recent book entitled *Backlash: The Undeclared War Against American Women,* Susan Faludi points out that many men today still resent women's progress in becoming independent personally and professionally. Faludi notes that a seven-year survey of American male attitudes in the 1980s found that no more than 5 to 10 percent of the men surveyed genuinely supported women's demands for independence and equality today.

Although some women view the Men's Movement as a backlash, many others see the Men's Movement as something that is good for both men and women. They see it as men's need to form a brotherhood for psychological support to protect their rights and personal freedoms as women formed support groups with other women to protect and advance their rights. They think, for example, that women should not automatically be given custody of children when a divorce occurs, and yet this is what often happens in the United States today. Finally, some authorities relate the development of the Men's Movement to the confusion created by the crisis of masculinity in contemporary society, and the many and changing images portrayed in the popular media of who and what real men are and how they are supposed to act. If you watch American movies, you might find yourself asking: Is the real man, for example, a sensitive guy like Dustin Hoffman's *Tootsie*? Is he an involved dad like Robin Williams' *Mrs. Doubtfire*, or the father played by Steve Martin in *Parenthood*? A macho man like Arnold Schwarzeneger plays in *The Terminator*, or is he more a caring nurturer like the man Schwarze-neger played in the movie *Kindergarten Cop*? Many men are searching for answers to this question and are attempting to find answers from the leaders of the Men's Movement.

What are the origins of this crisis of masculinity that poses problems for many men today? One of the historical reasons for the crisis, according to Robert Bly, a poet who is considered to be one of the founding fathers of the Men's Movement, is rooted in the changes that took place in North America as a result of the Industrial Revolution which occurred in the early to mid 1900s. When the Industrial Revolution began, the kinds of work that people did (that is, the kinds of work men did) changed for many Americans. Before the Civil War, 88 percent of American males were small farmers, independent artisans, or small businessmen. In these professions, the workers usually worked close to their homes. This meant that sons were constantly learning how to work and support themselves and their families by working alongside their fathers. By 1910, however, less then one third of all men in the United States were self-employed. Sociologist Michael Kimmel points out that even then, many men felt that the concept of manhood was being threatened (and was even vanishing) because men no longer worked their land or had control over their labor. Many never got to see the fruits of their labor, as farmers and craftsmen usually do. Many men in the post–Industrial Revolution era had become mere cogs in the machines of industrial America. In addition, the change from a farm to an industrial society meant that instead of supporting their families by working near their homes as farmers, craftsmen, or small business owners, the majority of men began working in factories or offices. Often the factories and offices were far from their homes, and men had to travel long distances to work. This meant that the men were not home, and the amount of time fathers spent with their sons was greatly reduced. Young boys, therefore, did not have their fathers around to act as role models. The effects of the Industrial Revolution continue into the present day, according to men in the Men's Movement, and they want to address the problems it has brought. For example, many people are concerned that men still have little say in the upbringing of their children.

The evolution of the Women's Movement had a profound effect on the development of the Men's Movement. As a result of the Women's Movement, more women are working outside the home, and many men are playing a more active role in family life and are taking on some of the tasks involved in child care and housework. Thirty to forty years ago, care of the home and children were almost exclusively the responsibility of women. In addition to these changes inside the home, men are today entering occupations that used to be considered women's jobs. More men are becoming nurses and teachers of young children. Other men are finding that they have more female colleagues and bosses at work than ever before, and they are having to adapt to women's styles of communication and management, which can differ considerably from those of men. At work, as well as at home, many men today in modern North American society have to play very different roles than their fathers did. They are, as a result, joining with other men in the Men's Movement, or they are reading books such as Robert Bly's *Iron John* to try to understand and cope with the roles expected of men in today's world.

So some of the reasons for the Men's Movement can be attributed to the changing roles brought about by the Women's Movement, to the Industrial Revolution and to men's desire to understand and affirm the concept of manhood.

Exactly what forms does the Men's Movement take, and what do men in the Men's Movement hope to achieve by being active in the movement? To begin with, the Men's Movement has no unified, monolithic philosophy. Although there are a number of unifying themes, there are also some interesting differences among the basic groups associated with the Men's Movement. Several writers who write about the Men's Movement have identified four basic groups of men active in the movement.

The first group is labeled the male feminists, and these men work for women's rights and equality between the sexes. Some of the men in this first group are vocal about blaming other men for much of the violence against women and for the inequality that exists between men and women in relationships and the job market. Not all members of the Men's Movement, however, consider this first group of men to be an integral part of the Men's Movement. To be sure, the other three groups focus more on men's issues than do the so-called male feminists.

The second orientation in the Men's Movement attracts men who join men's support groups to meet regularly and give and receive psychological support in dealing with problems created by the new roles they have to play at home and at work. These men are attempting to learn to better express their feelings and emotions, and to show sensitivity without being ashamed. A third group in the Men's Movement consists of men who want to get back the power they feel they have lost because of the advances made by women as a result of the Women's Movement and feminist causes. Finally, there is an approach to the movement called the mytho-poetic Men's Movement. The mytho-poetic Men's Movement is often identified with Robert Bly, the poet who wrote one of the most well-known books of the Men's Movement, *Iron John*. The men involved in this aspect of the Men's Movement believe that men should be initiated into manhood as men were initiated when people still lived in small tribes and bands in more ancient cultures. This group initiates men using mythology, poetry (hence the name mytho-poetic), and other rituals, such as dancing to explore and affirm the value of masculinity and masculine approaches to problem solving. Men who subscribe to this viewpoint worry that too much contact with women and too little contact with other men has turned men into weaklings or wimps.

So, the Men's Movement is very diverse. A man who wants to join the movement has many options of just how he will explore the question, "What does it mean to be a man in today's world?"

What do women think of the Men's Movement? Just as there are many different ways for men to approach the Men's Movement, there are many different opinions about the value and worth of the movement. Some women, especially many feminists, do not like the Men's Movement. They feel the Men's Movement is a backlash, and that it is an example of how men are trying to keep women from achieving equality by forming stronger "good old boy" (or male-only) networks and by advocating women's return to their roles of housewife and mother rather than business partner or competitor. However, some women, particularly those whose husbands are part of men's support groups or who have gone on men's weekend retreats, are glad that men are learning to express their emotions and getting support from other men. Barbara Brotman reports in an article in *The Chicago Tribune* that one woman she interviewed is glad her husband has joined the Men's Movement because she no longer feels that she alone is responsible for their family's emotional well-being. She and her husband now share that role and responsibility.

This has been only a brief introduction to some of the issues related to the Men's Movement. Because of many different perceptions concerning the goals and purposes of the movement, it is difficult to give a simple definition or draw a simple portrait of the movement. Perhaps it would be better to say that the Men's Movement is like a tree with many branches and many roots. The movement is much younger than the Women's Movement in one form or another; however, it is beginning to have substantial impact on many North American men and women, as these men and women adapt to their changing roles in American society as the year 2000 approaches.

LISTENING AND NOTETAKING SCRIPT

The Women's Movement has gained a lot of attention in recent years in North America and in countries around the world, as you heard in the last lecture. The Women's Movement has inspired many women to fight for equal rights and treatment in their homes, their personal relationships, and at work. It has also forced many women to examine and to rethink the roles they play in society. However, not only have women begun to examine and rethink the roles they play at home, at work, and in modern society as a whole, but men also have begun to examine and rethink the roles they play in society, and to examine and rethink the various and changing roles they must play at home and work today.

Men have also begun to react in both positive and negative ways to the new expectations they must meet at home and at work. Some men are adjusting well to the new roles they must play as more and more women enter the job market, and some men are pleased that their wives and partners have jobs outside the home. However, some of the role changes men are having to make to accommodate their working wives and girlfriends, as well as some of the new expectations concerning their masculinity, are causing some of them a good deal of stress, anger, and confusion. Some are even asking the question "What does it mean to be a real man in today's world?" Many are confused about how they should treat women, whether these women are their female colleagues at work, their friends, or their wives. Some feel they are no longer "king of the castle" at home. As a result of this confusion and unhappiness, a countermovement called the Men's Movement has sprung up alongside the Women's Movement in the United States. Men in the movement seek to provide one another with the support they need to cope with the stresses and strains of being a man in today's world, and to cope with the stresses and strains brought about by the professional advances made and the personal freedoms won by women in many countries over the past few decades.

Alright, let's take a break. Have you noticed that you're listening and taking notes for longer and longer periods of time? It takes a lot of concentration to do this, but you need to develop the ability to listen and take notes if you intend to listen to lectures at an English-speaking university. Let's see how you did on the initial section of the lecture.

The lecturer began by remarking that the Women's Movement inspired many women to fight for equal rights at work, in their personal relationships, and where else? (Pause.) Right, at work. At the same time, women have had to rethink the roles—and the changing roles—they play at home and at work. The lecturer then suggests that men, too, have had to examine and rethink the roles they must play at home and at work. Men have adjusted to the new roles they have to play. But it has not been easy for some men who must take on new roles as their wives and girlfriends have begun to work outside the home. The threat to their masculinity is making many men stressed, angry, and confused. The lecturer noted that some men are asking the question, "What does it mean to be a man in today's world?" and many don't know the answer to this question. Do you remember the reference to the man's castle? How did you note down the fact that men are concerned that they are no longer "king of the castle," and this fact makes them confused and unhappy? For this reason, men in the United States began the Men's Movement to give and get support. The support helps them cope with the stresses and strains that have occurred since women have made professional advances and gained freedoms throughout the world. Ok. Were you able to write down a few phrases that would help you rewrite the information with correctly spelled words at a later time? Ok. Let's go on to the next part.

Some women view the Men's Movement as a backlash against the professional advances they have made and personal freedoms they have won as a result of the Women's Movement. Many men (and many women, also) see the Men's Movement as men's need to form a brotherhood for psychological support, just as women have formed support groups with other women. Others see the Men's Movement as men's attempt and need to understand more fully what it means and takes to be a "real man" at the close of the 20th century, when traditional definitions of manhood are changing or are under attack in many countries around the world.

What words, phrases—and I hope they were abbreviated—or notations did you write down to capture the attitudes toward the Men's Movement? I'll repeat the critical ideas, and you check your notes. The speaker said that many women view the movement as a backlash. Some men and women view it as men's need to form a brotherhood for psychological support—like women did with their movement. Others view it as an attempt to better understand what it means and takes to be a real man—when traditional definitions of what it means to be a man are changing or under attack. Let's return to the lecture as the speaker begins to discuss some of the reasons for (or the catalysts for) the Men's Movement. The lecturer will speak for a longer amount of time than he has up until now. Are you ready for a long stretch of notetaking?

To begin this discussion of some of the catalysts for the Men's Movement, I will say a few words about why some women consider the Men's Movement a reaction against the Women's Movement—what the well-known author Susan Faludi calls the "backlash" against the Women's Movement. Ms. Faludi suggests that some men feel that women are becoming too independent and powerful today as a result of the professional advances they have made in the workplace and because of the personal freedoms they have gained in their family and personal relationships. She notes that the resentment of some men toward women's gaining power is not a recent phenomenon. More than 1,900 years ago, the women of Rome tried to repeal a law that forbade them from riding in horse-drawn chariots and from wearing multicolored dresses. In 195 B.C., the Roman senator Cato expressed the fear that the women of Rome had become so powerful that the independence of the men of Rome had been lost in their homes, and was being trampled underfoot in public. In her recent book entitled *Backlash: The Undeclared War Against american Women,* Susan Faludi points out that many men today still resent women's progress in becoming independent personally and professionally. Faludi notes that a seven-year survey of American male attitudes in the 1980s found that no more than 5 to 10 percent of the men surveyed genuinely supported women's demands for independence and equality today.

Although some women view the Men's Movement as a backlash, many others see the Men's Movement as something that is good for both men and women. They see it as men's need to form a brotherhood for psychological support to protect their rights and personal freedoms as women formed support groups with other women to protect and advance their rights. They think, for example, that women should not automatically be given custody of children when a divorce occurs, and yet this is what often happens in the United States today. Finally, some authorities relate the development of the Men's Movement to the confusion created by the crisis of masculinity in contemporary society, and the many and changing images portrayed in the popular media of who and what real men are and how they are supposed to act. If you watch American movies, you might find yourself asking: Is the real man, for example, a sensitive guy like Dustin Hoffman's *Tootsie*? Is he an involved dad like Robin Williams' *Mrs. Doubtfire*, or the father played by Steve Martin in *Parenthood*? A macho man like Arnold Schwarzeneger plays in *The Terminator*, or is he more a caring nurturer like the man Schwarzeneger played in the movie *Kindergarten Cop*? Many men are searching for answers to this question and are attempting to find answers from the leaders of the Men's Movement.

The lecturer started off by listing some of the catalysts for the Men's Movement and why women view the movement as a reaction against the Women's Movement.

Some men feel that women are too independent and powerful today as a result of professional advances they have made and the personal freedoms they have won. Resentment against women is not new, the speaker said. In ancient Rome, for example, women were forbidden from riding in horse-drawn chariots and from wearing multicolored dresses more than 1900 years ago, and they tried to have these laws repealed. The author Susan Faludi in her book entitled Backlash: The Undeclared War Against American Women, *believes that many men today resent women's personal and professional independence. She claims in her book that no more than 5 to*

10 percent of the men surveyed genuinely support women's demands for independence and equality.

At this point, the lecturer changes from talking about the phenomenon of backlash to describing (1) how the movement functions as psychological support for men equivalent to the support women have received from the Women's Movement, and (2) how the movement helps men cope with the confusion created by the changing images of men in popular media. The speaker mentions a number of images in popular movies, like Mrs. Doubtfire, The Terminator, *and* Kindergarten Cop. *Did you write down the types of movies these are? Let's now finish the lecture. You will take notes without any assistance given for this next and final segment of the lecture. Ready?*

What are the origins of this crisis of masculinity that poses problems for many men today? One of the historical reasons for the crisis, according to Robert Bly, a poet who is considered to be one of the founding fathers of the Men's Movement, is rooted in the changes that took place in North America as a result of the Industrial Revolution which occurred in the early to mid 1900s. When the Industrial Revolution began, the kinds of work that people did (that is, the kinds of work men did) changed for many Americans. Before the Civil War, 88 percent of American males were small farmers, independent artisans, or small businessmen. In these professions, the workers usually worked close to their homes. This meant that sons were constantly learning how to work and support themselves and their families by working alongside their fathers. By 1910, however, less then one third of all men in the United States were self-employed. Sociologist Michael Kimmel points out that even then, many men felt that the concept of manhood was being threatened (and was even vanishing) because men no longer worked their land or had control over their labor. Many never got to see the fruits of their labor, as farmers and craftsmen usually do. Many men in the post–Industrial Revolution era had become mere cogs in the machines of industrial America. In addition, the change from a farm to an industrial society meant that instead of supporting their families by working near their homes as farmers, craftsmen, or small business owners, the majority of men began working in factories or offices. Often the factories and offices were far from their homes, and men had to travel long distances to work. This meant that the men were not home, and the amount of time fathers spent with their sons was greatly reduced. Young boys, therefore, did not have their fathers around to act as role models. The effects of the Industrial Revolution continue into the present day, according to men in the Men's Movement, and they want to address the problems it has brought. For example, many people are concerned that men still have little say in the upbringing of their children.

The evolution of the Women's Movement had a profound effect on the development of the Men's Movement. As a result of the Women's Movement, more women are working outside the home, and many men are playing a more active role in family life and are taking on some of the tasks involved in child care and housework. Thirty to forty years ago, care of the home and children were almost exclusively the responsibility of women. In addition to these changes inside the home, men are today entering occupations that used to be considered women's jobs. More men are becoming nurses and teachers of young children. Other men are finding that they have more female colleagues and bosses at work than ever before, and they are having to adapt to women's styles of communication and management, which can differ considerably from those of men. At work, as well as at home, many men today in modern North American society have to play very different roles than their fathers did. They are, as a result, joining with other men in the Men's Movement, or they are reading books such as Robert Bly's *Iron John* to try to understand and cope with the roles expected of men in today's world.

So some of the reasons for the Men's Movement can be attributed to the changing roles brought about by the Women's Movement, to the Industrial Revolution, and to men's desire to understand and affirm the concept of manhood.

Exactly what forms does the Men's Movement take, and what do men in the Men's Movement hope to achieve by being active in the movement? To begin with, the Men's Movement has no unified, monolithic philosophy. Although there are a number of unifying themes, there are also some interesting differences among the basic groups associated with the Men's Movement. Several writers who write about the Men's Movement have identified four basic groups of men active in the movement.

The first group is labeled the male feminists, and these men work for women's rights and equality between the sexes. Some of the men in this first group are vocal about blaming other men for much of the violence against women and for the inequality that exists between men and women in relationships and the job market. Not all members of the Men's Movement, however, consider this first group of men to be an integral part of the Men's Movement. To be sure, the other three groups focus more on men's issues than do the so-called male feminists.

The second orientation in the Men's Movement attracts men who join men's support groups to meet regularly and give and receive psychological support in dealing with problems created by the new roles they have to play at home and at work. These men are attempting to learn to better express their feelings and emotions, and to show sensitivity without being ashamed. A third group in the Men's Movement consists of men who want to get back the power they feel they have lost because of the advances made by women as a result of the Women's Movement and feminist causes. Finally, there is an approach to the movement called the mytho-poetic Men's Movement. The mytho-poetic Men's Movement is often identified with Robert Bly, the poet who wrote one of the most well-known books of the Men's Movement, *Iron John*. The men involved in this aspect of the Men's Movement believe that men should be initiated into manhood as men were initiated when people still lived in small tribes and bands in more ancient cultures. This group initiates men using mythology, poetry (hence the name mytho-poetic), and other rituals, such as dancing to explore and affirm the value of masculinity and masculine approaches to problem solving. Men who subscribe to this viewpoint worry that too much contact with women and too little contact with other men has turned men into weaklings or wimps.

So, the Men's Movement is very diverse. A man who wants to join the movement has many options of just how he will explore the question, "What does it mean to be a man in today's world?"

What do women think of the Men's Movement? Just as there are many different ways for men to approach the Men's Movement, there are many different opinions about the value and worth of the movement. Some women, especially many feminists, do not like the Men's Movement. They feel the Men's Movement is a backlash, and that it is an example of how men are trying to keep women from achieving equality by forming stronger "good old boy" (or male-only) networks and by advocating women's return to their roles of housewife and mother rather than business partner or competitor. However, some women, particularly those whose husbands are part of men's support groups or who have gone on men's weekend retreats, are glad that men are learning to express their emotions and getting support from other men. Barbara Brotman reports in an article in *The Chicago Tribune* that one woman she interviewed is glad her husband has joined the Men's Movement because she no longer feels that she alone is responsible for their family's emotional well-being. She and her husband now share that role and responsibility.

This has been only a brief introduction to some of the issues related to the Men's Movement. Because of many different perceptions concerning the goals and purposes of the movement, it is difficult to give a simple definition or draw a simple portrait of the movement. Perhaps it would be better to say that the Men's Movement is like a tree with many branches and many roots. The movement is much younger than the Women's Movement in one form or another; however, it is beginning to have substantial impact on many North American men and women, as these men and women adapt to their changing roles in American society as the year 2000 approaches.

Well, how did you do? Take the time to check your notes with a classmate. Look at your notes and present the information in the final section of the lecture to him or her. Share the task. You present the information in one segment of the lecture, and then allow your classmate to present the information in the next section. If you missed any of the information, you will have an opportunity to complete your notes as you listen to your classmate.

Unit 5

Intercultural Communication: The Influence of Language, Culture, and Gender

Lecture 9
Classroom Communication: Language and Culture in the Classroom

ORIENTATION LISTENING SCRIPT

Today's lecture deals with the topic of language, culture, and communication in the North American classroom. Samovar and Porter, in their book *Intercultural Communication*, define "communication" as a form of human behavior that results from a need to interact with other human beings.

As a result of this need, we send verbal and nonverbal messages to communicate with both friends and strangers. Communication can take the form of talk, or it can take the form of gestures, or nonverbal signals, of one kind or another. The talk or signals send messages that communicate a person's thoughts, feelings, and intentions to others. Many scholars study the general topic of communication, in general, and speech communication, specifically, in order to learn how individuals send and interpret messages. A number of these scholars conduct research on the topic of intercultural communication. That is, they study communication between people from different cultures. One area of research in intercultural communication is the study of the influence of the setting, or environment, on the success and/or failure of communication. In this lecture, I will be talking about one specific aspect of intercultural communication; that is intercultural communication that takes place in the classroom. This information is taken from a book chapter written by Janis Andersen and Robert Powell entitled "Intercultural Communication and the Classroom." It appeared in Samovar and Porter's edited book *Intercultural Communication.*

When you are asked to picture a classroom in your mind's eye, what do you see? You probably see a classroom that is familiar to you and that would be familiar to students from your culture. However, not everyone will see the same picture in their minds. Although many people have similar images of what a classroom looks like in their mind's eye, their culture greatly influences the way they view the teacher-student environment, and culture also influences how a person understands the ways in which information is taught and learned in the classroom. Culture also plays an important role in determining how teachers and students communicate in the classroom. In this lecture, I'll give you a few examples of some of the ways that culture affects this communication. The "classroom" as we know it, by the way, is a relatively recent innovation, according to Janis Andersen and Robert Powell. Great teachers like Socrates, Plato, Aristotle, and Confucius taught without the benefit of a blackboard, chalk, desks, and the standard comforts (or discomforts) of a classroom building. But let me return to the main topic of this lecture—the influence of culture on behavior and communication between teacher and students in the classroom.

If you have come from another culture to study in North America, you may already have noticed that teachers and students in American universities interact and communicate in the classroom in ways that differ from how teachers and students communicate in your home culture. It's culture that influences and establishes these interactions and communication patterns. Of course, culture is a term that is used in many different ways. Basically, culture provides us with a system of knowledge that allows us to communicate with others and teaches us how to interpret their verbal and nonverbal behavior. Culture influences and establishes how people interact with one another (or do not interact with one another). In particular, culture influences the rituals that take place in the classroom setting, and it influences the ways students participate in the classroom discourse. It also influences the esteem in which teachers are held.

Rituals are systematic procedures used to perform a certain act or to communicate a certain message. In some countries, when a teacher enters the classroom, the students ritually stand up. In the United States, a classroom ritual occurs when a student raises her hand to signal to the teacher that she knows the answer to a question. This is not a universal classroom ritual to signal intent to answer a question, however. Jamaican students snap or flap their fingers to signal that they want to answer a question that has been posed. In some college- and graduate-level seminars in North American universities, students do not make any physical signs when they want to speak; they state their ideas whenever they feel the urge or when they feel it is appropriate. This sort of classroom behavior is especially confusing to students from cultures in which there are no rituals for attracting the teacher's attention because the student is not expected to participate in the class at all.

This brings us to the issue of classroom participation. North American students of European origin are usually more talkative in class and more willing to share their opinions than students of Native American heritage or from Asian backgrounds. This brings us to the issue of classroom participation. This difference is directly related to cultural values about learning and education, and classroom behavior. Euro-American students' culture teaches them that learning is shaped and helped by their talk and active participation in exploring or discussing issues. Asian students, however, are generally taught that they will learn best by listening to and absorbing the knowledge being given to them by the teacher. In their article "Culture and Classroom Communication," Janis Andersen and Robert Powell point out that some cultures do not have a way for students to signal a desire to talk to a teacher; in these cultures, students speak out only after the teacher has spoken to them. Most classroom interaction in Vietnam is tightly controlled by the teacher, according to Andersen and Powell.

The esteem in which teachers are held also varies culturally. The Vietnamese have a great deal of respect for their instructors and consider them to be honored members of society, according to researchers Samovar and Porter. They see instructors as symbols of learning and culture. In Germany, students value the personal opinions of their instructors, and it is not customary to disagree with or contradict teachers. Israeli students, on the other hand, can criticize an instructor if they feel that he or she is wrong about some issue or information, according to Samovar and Porter.

There are many other ways that culture can affect interaction and communication between teachers and students in the classroom. This lecture has covered differences in only one or two classroom rituals and pointed out the difference in the ways students from different cultures participate or communicate with the teacher during class. However, from this brief consideration of classroom communication, you should begin to see that learning a language involves more than studying the vocabulary, idioms, and the grammar of the language. There are many culture-specific patterns of communication, such as the patterns of classroom communication, that a student of a second or foreign language must also learn.

LISTENING AND NOTETAKING SCRIPT

Today's lecture deals with the topic of language, culture, and communication in the North American classroom. Samovar and Porter, in their book *Intercultural Communication,* define communication as a form of human behavior that results from a need to interact with other human beings. As a result of this need, we send verbal and nonverbal messages to communicate with both friends and strangers. Communication can take the form of talk, or it can take the form of gestures, or nonverbal signals, of one kind or another. The talk or signals send messages that communicate a person's thoughts, feelings, and intentions to others. Many scholars study the topic of communication, in general, and speech communication, specifically, in order to learn how individuals send and interpret messages. A number of these scholars conduct research on the topic of intercultural communication. That is, they study communication between people from different cultures. One area of research in intercultural communication is the study of the influence of the setting, or environment on the success and/or the failure of the communication. In this lecture, I'll be talking about one specific aspect of intercultural communication; that is the intercultural communication that takes place in the classroom. The information is taken from a book chapter written by Janis Andersen and Robert Powell. The chapter entitled "Intercultural Communication and the Classroom" appeared in Samovar and Porter's edited book *Intercultural Communication.*

If I ask you to picture a classroom in your mind's eye, what do you see? You probably see a classroom that is familiar to you and that would be familiar to students from your country and culture. However, not everyone will see the same picture in their minds. Although many people have similar images of what a classroom looks like in their mind's eye, their culture greatly influences the way they view the teacher-student environment. Culture also influences how a person understands the ways in which information is taught and learned in the classroom. Culture also plays an important role in determining how teachers and students communicate in the classroom. In this lecture, I'll give you a few examples of some of the ways culture affects that communication. The classroom is a relatively recent invention, by the way, according to Janis Andersen and Robert Powell. Great teachers like Socrates, Plato, Aristotle, and Confucius taught without the benefit of a blackboard, chalk, desks, and the standard comforts (or discomforts) of a classroom building. But I'm getting off the topic. Let me return to the main topic of this lecture—the influence of culture on classroom behavior and communication between teacher and students in the classroom.

Let's take a brief break from listening and notetaking to check your notes and give you an opportunity to see how you're doing so far. I'll limit my mentoring to providing an outline of the lecture and asking a few questions which you should be able to answer by looking in your notes.

The speaker opened the lecture with a definition of the term "communication." Check your notes. Can you define the term? You don't have to define it in the exact words the speaker used; you can paraphrase slightly as long as you can provide a definition of the term that captures the meaning given by

Samovar and Porter. Did you note their names, even if you didn't get the spelling correct? (Pause.) Ok. The speaker next mentioned why people communicate—they have a need to interact with other human beings—and how they communicate—with verbal and non-verbal messages. Is there anything else you included in your notes about the first few points made by the lecturer? (Pause.) Ok. What did the lecturer discuss next? It involved the research of speech communication scholars and what some of them study. What do some of these speech communication scholars study? Right. Intercultural communication and, more specifically, the influence of the communication setting (e.g., the classroom) and the success and/or the failure of the communication. At this point, the lecturer started to get more specific about the kind of intercultural communication he would be dealing with. Check your notes. What was it? I'm confident that you can answer that question. Let me continue. The next topic dealt with was the classroom and culture. The speaker began this section of the lecture asking you to get a picture in your mind's eye of a classroom. Did you note this? Why or why not? What was the point of using the mental picture technique? You have to decide what you don't need to take down in your notes, and this example was something that could have been omitted, but the important point of why it was used should have found its way into your notes. Can you find the answer to this question in your notes? Let's return to the lecture.

If you have come from another country and a different culture to study in an American university, you may already have noticed that teachers and students in American universities interact and communicate in the classroom in ways that differ from how teachers and students communicate in your home culture. It's culture that influences and establishes these interactions and communication patterns, as I said before. Of course, culture is a term that is used in many different ways. Basically, culture provides us with a system of knowledge that helps us to communicate with others. This system of knowledge teaches us how to interpret other people's verbal and nonverbal behavior and their use of symbols. Culture influences and even establishes the ways people interact with one another (or do not interact with one another), and therefore, culture influences how teachers and students communicate in the classroom. In particular, culture influences the classroom rituals that take place in the classroom setting, and it influences the ways students participate in the classroom discourse—that's the classroom talk and discussion. Culture also influences the esteem and respect in which teachers are held.

Just what exactly are "rituals"? I'll give you a dictionary definition, to begin with. "Rituals" are systematic procedures used to perform a certain act or to communicate a certain message. For example, there are many rituals connected with eating, both how and what we eat. Well, there are many rituals associated with teaching and learning, and education in general. In some countries, for example, when a teacher enters the classroom, the students all stand up ritualistically. This is not usually what happens in the U.S. Let me give you another example of a classroom ritual. In the United States, a classroom ritual occurs whenever a student raises her hand to signal that she knows the answer to a question that the teacher has asked. A student's raising a hand is not a universal classroom ritual to signal intent to answer a question, however. In Jamaica, students snap or flap their fingers to signal to the teacher that they want to answer a question. In some college- and graduate-level seminars in North American universities, students do not make any physical signs, such as raising their hands, when they want to speak. Whenever they feel the urge to speak, or when they feel it is appropriate to comment, they just start talking. This sort of classroom behavior on the part of American students is especially confusing to students from cultures that do not encourage students to participate in class discussion. Some cultures don't have a "systematic procedure," or "a ritual," for attracting the teacher's attention because students are not expected to participate vocally in the class at all.

This brings us to the issue of classroom participation. Many people have observed that North American students, especially those of European origin, tend to be more talkative in class and appear to be more willing to express their opinions than students of Native American heritage or students from Asian backgrounds. This difference in the patterns of classroom participation is related to the cultural values the three groups have about learning and education, and about classroom behavior. Euro-American students' culture, for example, teaches them that learning is shaped and helped by their talking and by their actively exploring or discussing issues with the teacher or professor. Asian students, however, are often taught that they will learn best by listening to their professors and by absorbing the knowledge being given to them. In their article on "Culture and Classroom Communication," Janis Andersen and Robert Powell point out that some cultures do not have a way for students to signal a desire to talk to a teacher during class; in these cultures, students speak out only after the teacher has spoken to them. Most classroom interaction in Vietnam, for example, is tightly controlled by the teacher, according to Andersen and Powell.

The esteem in which teachers are held, also varies from culture to culture. Samovar and Porter note that the Vietnamese have a great deal of respect for their teachers and consider them to be honored members of Vietnamese society. The Vietnamese and many other Asian peoples see the teacher . . . the instructor . . . the professor . . . as the very "symbol" of learning and culture. In Germany, students value the professional and even the personal opinion of the instructor, and it is not customary to disagree with or contradict a teacher during class. Israeli students, on the other hand, can criticize outright any teacher they feel is wrong about some issue or who they believe has provided incorrect information, according to Samovar and Porter.

There are many, many ways in which culture can affect interaction and communication between teachers and students in the classroom. I have discussed differences in how students get the teacher's attention during class, and I've pointed out the differences in the ways students from various cultures participate during the class, or communicate with the teacher during class. However, from this brief consideration of classroom communication, you should begin to see that learning a language involves more than learning the vocabulary, idioms, and the grammar of the language. It means learning many culture-specific patterns of communication, such as the patterns of classroom communication, that a student of a second or foreign language must also absorb and learn. If you are to succeed in communicating in a second-language classroom, you need to learn not only the language spoken in the classroom, but also the expected procedures of classroom participation and communication, that is, the rituals of language, culture, and communication. Let's end our communication, at this point.

Let me interrupt for a moment. I'll mention the main topics of the section of the lecture you just heard. Check your notes to be sure that you have this list of major topics:

1. *Classroom rituals—can you define the term "ritual"? Can you give the examples of rituals that were mentioned?*

2. *Classroom participation—can you describe the differences between North American and Asian students' participation in class? Are you using your memory or your notes to answer the question? What did the lecturer say about Vietnamese classroom participation patterns?*

3. *The esteem in which teachers are held. Look at your notes and see whether you can synopsize the information presented about this topic.*

Finally, what was the final topic dealt with? Did you write it down and can you decode the notes you took to reconstruct the information? If you can, you're making progress in developing your listening comprehension and notetaking skills.

LECTURE 10
GENDER AND COMMUNICATION: MALE-FEMALE CONVERSATION AS CROSS-CULTURAL COMMUNICATION

ORIENTATION LISTENING SCRIPT

In the first lecture, you heard about the relationship between culture and classroom communication. In this lecture, I'll talk about another variable that affects human communication. That variable is gender. Gender is the social identity that men and women learn as they grow up in a culture. For example, boys learn to be "masculine" and girls learn to be "feminine" as they grow to be men and women. Researchers have shown that men and women (and boys and girls, for that matter) communicate in quite different ways and in different amounts, depending on the situation the speakers find themselves in, and the reason or reasons they're communicating with other people.

Many cultures actually encourage men and women to talk differently and in different amounts, and these patterns for communicating are learned when men and women are young boys and girls. Children learn how to talk to other children or adults, and how to have conversations, not only from their parents but also from their peers—from other boys and girls their age. In her best-selling book *You Just Don't Understand*, Deborah Tannen points out that, although American boys and girls often play together, they spend *most* of their time playing in same-sex groups. She also points out that boys and girls *do* play some games together, but their favorite games are very often quite different. Tannen and other researchers on this topic have found that young boys, say ages 8 through 12, tend to play outside the house rather than in the house, and they play in large groups that are hierarchically structured. The group of boys generally has a leader who tells the other boys what to do and how to do it. It is by giving orders and making the other boys play by the rules that boys achieve higher or more dominant status in their play group. Boys also achieve status by taking "center stage." They take center stage by talking a lot; they give orders and commands; they tell a lot of stories and jokes. They command attention by dominating conversations and by interrupting other boys who are speaking. The researchers also found that boys' games often have clear winners and losers and elaborate systems of rules.

Researchers found that girls play different kinds of games and abide by different rules when playing their games. In addition, girls in groups use different patterns of communication and different styles of communication when playing together. Tannen and her colleagues have found that young girls often play in small groups or in pairs. They play less often in large groups or teams outside the home. Girls' play is not so hierarchically ordered as boys' play is. In their most frequent games, like hopscotch and jump rope, every girl gets a chance to play hopscotch or to jump rope. In many of their play activities, such as playing house, there are no "winners" or "losers." Researchers also found that girls usually don't give many direct orders or commands to their playmates; they express their preferences as suggestions, according to Tannen. Girls often say to their playmates, "Let's do this . . . or that." Boys, on the other hand, are more direct in ordering their playmates to do this or that. Tannen is quick to point out that North American boys as well as girls want to get their way, and want other children to do what they want them to do; however, the boys and girls try to get their playmates to do what they want them to do in different ways. Another well-known researcher, Marjorie Harness Goodwin, compared boys and girls engaged in two task-oriented activities. The boys were making slingshots in preparation for a fight. The girls were making jewelry; they were making rings for their fingers. Goodwin noted that the boys' activity group was hierarchically arranged. The "leader" told the other boys what to do and how to do it. The girls making the rings were more egalitarian. Everyone made suggestions about how to make the rings, and the girls tended to listen and accept the suggestions of the other girls in the group.

Goodwin is not suggesting that girls never engage in some of the communication and management behaviors boys engage in. In fact, in another study, she found that when girls play house, the girl who plays the mother gives orders to the girls who play the children. Girls seem to give orders to their peers less often than boys do when they play. The girls are practicing parent-child relationships in the game of playing house. It's very likely that when little boys play their games, they are also practicing the masculine roles they're expected to assume when they grow up.

As a result of our cultural upbringing, we learn norms of behavior and patterns of communication that are often gender-based, and sometimes gender-biased. We also develop stereotypes about how and how much males and females, that is, girls and boys or women and men should—and do—communicate. However, researchers have shown that many of these stereotypes actually turn out to be quite wrong.

Well, one of the most common stereotypes that many people hold is the idea that women talk a lot, perhaps too much, and that they are always interrupting or trying to get "center stage" when someone else is talking. There is, in fact, a proverb that reinforces this idea. It states that "foxes are all tail and women are all tongue." Actually, recent research on the influence of gender on communication has shown the exact opposite to be true in many instances!

Researchers have found that men usually produce more talk than women and are more likely to interrupt another speaker than women will—particularly in public settings, such as business meetings. So although women *are believed* to talk more than men, study after study has shown that it is men who talk more at meetings, in mixed-group discussions, and in classrooms where girls or young women sit next to boys or young men. And this finding holds even for communicative interactions between very educated and successful professional men and women, such as professors, for example. Deborah Tannen, in her book *You Just Don't Understand*, cites a study conducted by Barbara and Gene Eakins, who tape-recorded and studied seven university faculty meetings. They found that, with one exception, men professors spoke more often and, without exception, for a longer period of time than the women professors did. The men took center stage and talked from 10.66 seconds to 17.07 seconds, while the women talked from 3 to 10 seconds, on the average. Tannen points out that the women's longest turns were still shorter than the men's shortest turns. Angela Simeone reports another example of this phenomenon in her book, *Academic Women*. She found that women professors talk at departmental meetings less often than their male colleagues do. When asked how often they spoke at departmental meetings, 46 percent of the American men professors reported that they spoke often at these meetings, but only 15 percent of the women professors reported that they spoke often at departmental meetings.

Perhaps it is our social concept of what is feminine and what is masculine that reinforces the stereotype that women talk more than men, and even causes these different patterns of communication. Maybe a woman is labeled talkative or is criticized for interrupting if she does these things at all, because our culture—as well as many other cultures—teaches that women should be quiet if they want to be "feminine." Perhaps masculine culture encourages boys and men to dominate talk and to interrupt more often, and males who talk a lot and interrupt often are not criticized for doing so. These differences in the patterns of communication and styles of communicating are studied by researchers who study the effects of gender on communication. They study these effects in order to understand why misunderstandings occur between men and women in conversation. Often, it's because their styles and patterns of conversation are so different. It is important that we learn to recognize these differences so that we can learn to communicate better with people of the other gender. It is important to emphasize that these differences may be specific to North American culture. Gender can affect communication in even more and stronger ways in some other cultures. In Zulu culture, for example, a wife is forbidden to say any words that sound like the names of her father-in-law or brothers. This means she must paraphrase these words, and she is expected to do so.

So you see, cultural differences are not the only things that affect language and communication. Language is affected by gender as well. I'm sure you can think of many ways that gender affects communication between men and women in your own culture.

LISTENING AND NOTETAKING SCRIPT

In the first lecture, you heard about the relationship between culture and classroom communication. In this lecture, I'll talk about another variable that affects human communication. That variable is gender. Gender is the social identity that men and women learn as they grow up in a culture. For example, boys learn to be "masculine" and girls learn to be "feminine" as they grow to be men and women. Researchers have shown that men and women (and boys and girls, for that matter), communicate in quite different ways and in different amounts, depending on the situation the speakers find themselves in, and the reason or reasons they're communicating with other people.

Many cultures actually encourage men and women to talk differently and in different amounts, and these patterns for communicating are learned when men and women are young boys and girls. Children learn how to talk to other children or adults, and how to have conversations, not only from their parents but also from their peers—from other boys and girls their age. In her best-selling book *You Just Don't Understand*, Deborah Tannen points out that, although American boys and girls often play together, they spend *most* of their time playing in same-sex groups. She also points out that boys and girls *do* play some games together, but their favorite games are very often quite different. Tannen and other researchers on this topic have found that young boys, say ages 8 through 12, tend to play outside the house rather than in the house, and they play in large groups that are hierarchically structured. The group of boys generally has a leader who tells the other boys what to do and how to do it. It is by giving orders and making the other boys play by the rules that boys achieve higher or more dominant status in their play group. Boys also achieve status by taking "center stage." They take center stage by talking a lot; they give orders and commands; they tell a lot of stories and jokes. They command attention by dominating conversations and by interrupting other boys who are speaking. The researchers also found that boys' games often have clear winners and losers and elaborate systems of rules.

Researchers found that girls play different kinds of games and abide by different rules when playing their games. In addition, girls in groups use different patterns of communication and different styles of communication when playing together. Tannen and her colleagues have found that young girls often play in small groups or in pairs. They play less often in large groups or teams outside the home. Girls' play is not so hierarchically ordered as boys' play is. In their most frequent games, like hopscotch and jump rope, every girl gets a chance to play hopscotch or to jump rope. In many of their play activities, such as playing house, there are no "winners" or "losers." Researchers also found that girls usually don't give many direct orders or commands to their playmates; they express their preferences as suggestions, according to Tannen. Girls often say to their playmates, "Let's do this . . . or that." Boys, on the other hand, are more direct in ordering their playmates to do this or that. Tannen is quick to point out that North American boys as well as girls want to get their way, and want other children to do what they want them to do; however, the boys and girls try to get their playmates to do what they want them to do in different ways. Another well-known researcher, Marjorie Harness Goodwin, compared boys and girls engaged in two task-oriented activities. The boys were making slingshots in preparation for a fight. The girls were making jewelry; they were making rings for their fingers. Goodwin noted that the boys' activity group was hierarchically arranged. The "leader" told the other boys what to do and how to do it. The girls making the rings were more egalitarian. Everyone made suggestions about how to make the rings, and the girls tended to listen and accept the suggestions of the other girls in the group.

Goodwin is not suggesting that girls never engage in some of the communication and management behaviors boys engage in. In fact, in another study, she found that when girls play house, the girl who plays the mother gives orders to the girls who play the children. Girls seem to give orders to their peers less often than boys do when they play. The girls are practicing parent-child relationships in the game of playing house. It's very likely that when little boys play their games, they are also practicing the masculine roles they're expected to assume when they grow up.

In this lecture, the lecturer dealt with two major topics and a number of subtopics. She began talking about two things that influence gender and communication: the fact that gender is learned, and the fact that men and women learn to communicate in different ways and amounts, depending on the situation and the reason for talking or communicating. Next, the lecturer talked about Tannen's observations concerning children's communication patterns at play. What examples did she give that show how boys and girl play differently? How did you list these differences in your notes? (Pause.) The listing doesn't have to be as complete as the outline you looked at the first time you heard the lecture. Finally, did you have a chance to write down some information about the Goodwin study, which compared boys making weapons for a fight with girls playing house? Check your notes, and if you want to add any information, go ahead and add it in note form. Let's continue. The speaker takes up the topic of stereotypes, sometimes mistaken stereotypes, about gender and communication in the next part of the lecture and talks about the results of a research study by Eakins and Eakins. Are you ready to continue listening and developing your notetaking abilities?

As a result of our cultural upbringing, we learn norms of behavior and patterns of communication that are often gender-based, and sometimes gender-biased. We also develop stereotypes about how and how much males and females, that is, girls and boys or women and men should—and do—communicate. However, researchers have shown that many of these stereotypes actually turn out to be quite wrong.

Well, one of the most common stereotypes that many people hold is the idea that women talk a lot, perhaps too much, and that they are always interrupting or trying to get "center stage" when someone else is talking. There is, in fact, a proverb that reinforces this idea. It states that "foxes are all tail and women are all tongue." Actually, recent research on the influence of gender on communication has shown the exact opposite to be true in many instances!

Researchers have found that men usually produce more talk than women and are more likely to interrupt another speaker than women will—particularly in public settings, such as business meetings. So although women *are believed* to talk more than men, study after study has shown that it is men who talk more at meetings, in mixed-group discussions, and in classrooms where girls or young women sit next to boys or young men. And this finding holds even for communicative interactions between very educated and successful professional men and women, such as professors, for example. Deborah Tannen, in her book *You Just Don't Understand*, cites a study conducted by Barbara and Gene Eakins, who tape-recorded and studied seven university faculty meetings. They found that, with one exception, men professors spoke more often and, without exception, for a longer period of time than the women professors did. The men took center stage and talked from 10.66 seconds to 17.07 seconds, while the women talked from 3 to 10 seconds, on the average. Tannen points out that the women's longest turns were still shorter than the men's shortest turns. Angela Simeone reports another example of this phenomenon in her book, *Academic Women*. She found that women professors talk at departmental meetings less often than their male colleagues do. When asked how often they spoke at departmental meetings, 46 percent of the American men professors reported that they spoke often at these meetings, but only 15 percent of the women professors reported that they spoke often at departmental meetings.

Perhaps it is our social concept of what is feminine and what is masculine that reinforces the stereotype that women talk more than men, and even causes these different patterns of communication. Maybe a woman is labeled talkative or is criticized for interrupting if she does these things at all, because our culture—as well as many other cultures—teaches that women should be quiet if they want to be "feminine." Perhaps masculine culture encourages boys and men to dominate talk and to interrupt more often, and males who talk a lot and interrupt often are not criticized for doing so. These differences in the patterns of communication and styles of communicating are studied by researchers who study the effects of gender on communication. They study these effects in order to understand why misunderstandings occur between men and women in conversation. Often, it's because their styles and patterns of conversation are so different. It is important that we learn to recognize these differences so that we can learn to communicate better with people of the other gender. It is important to emphasize that these differences may be specific to North American culture. Gender can affect communication in even more and stronger ways in some other cultures. In Zulu culture, for example, a wife is forbidden to say any words that sound like the names of her father-in-law or brothers. This means she must paraphrase these words, and she is expected to do so.

So you see, cultural differences are not the only things that affect language and communication. Language is affected by gender as well. I'm sure you can think of many ways that gender affects communication between men and women in your own culture.

Well, let me sum up the major points made in this final part of the lecture for your note check. The lecturer noted that a common stereotype is that women talk a lot—too much, in fact. However, research shows that men actually talk more—especially in public settings. The lecturer made reference to the research study that showed that even university men and women engaged in different patterns and amounts of talk during faculty meetings. Did you note the statistics that demonstrate that men professors talked longer and more often than women professors? Did that fact surprise you? There were several authors mentioned during this part of the lecture. How did you handle taking notes on the names that were used? It is likely that you'll have to review your notes after a lecture and fill in what you missed. Names may prove to be a problem for your notetaking, but practice will help you develop familiarity with the sound and pattern of names used in references. Let me repeat the title of the books the lecturer mentioned: Tannen's **You Just Don't Understand** *and Simeone's* **Academic Women.**

Finally, can you tell me—from looking at your notes—what information the lecturer ended the lecture with? Well, it has something to do with the different social concept of what feminine and masculine are in our society—or should I say "societies"? We need to understand why men and women talk more or less, and what makes them talk more or less. We need to understand that culture dictates how, why, and when men and women communicate as they do—or as they don't. Take the Zulu culture, for example. Take my culture or your culture, for example. But that is a topic for another day and another lecture.

UNIT 1

History: The Passing of Time and Civilizations

LECTURE 1
THE END OF AN EMPIRE: MONTEZUMA AND CORTES

1. The Aztecs built their empire between 1423 and 1440.

2. The Aztec capital city was called Tenochtitlan.

3. 300,000 people lived in Tenochtitlan.

4. Montezuma believed Cortes to be the god Quetzalcoatl.

5. The Spaniards entered Tenochtitlan in November of 1519.

6. *La noche triste* was June 30, 1520.

7. The Aztecs thought the Spaniards were half-man and half-animal because they rode on horses, and the Aztecs had never seen horses.

8. The Indian woman who translated for Cortes was called La Malinche and also, Doña Marina.

9. La Malinche spoke the languages of the Aztecs and the Mayans. Presumably she learned English also, but the lecturer does not say so.

10. The Spaniards were able to capture Tenochtitlan because (a) the Aztecs were afraid Cortes was a supernatural god, Quetzalcoatl; (b) the Spaniards had superior weapons; (c) Cortes convinced many Indians who wanted Aztec rule to end to join him; and (d) the Spaniards wanted to collect as much gold and silver as possible.

11. The Indian and European cultures fused to form the culture of the Republic of Mexico.

LECTURE 2
THE EGYPTIAN PYRAMIDS: HOUSES OF ETERNITY

1. The Egyptian Empire lasted for more than 3,000 years.

2. At least 30 consecutive dynasties ruled ancient Egypt.

3. The pyramids were tombs or burial places for Egyptian pharoahs and their families.

4. Grave goods included clothing, food, furniture, weapons and servants.

5. The first type of pyramid is called a mastaba.

6. King Zoser's pyramid was the first step pyramid.

7. The architect Imhotep built King Zoser's step pyramid.

8. The three great pyramids are located in Giza.

9. The Greeks called King Khufu "Cheops."

10. King Khufu's pyramids used approximately 2,300,000 limestone blocks.

11. Menkaure's pyramid is 62.5 meters high.

12. Thutmose I had his tomb dug out of a rock far from the city to try to hide his grave from grave robbers.

UNIT 2
PORTRAITS OF POLITICAL LEADERS: MYSTIC VERSUS REALITY

LECTURE 3
JOHN F. KENNEDY: PROMISE AND TRAGEDY

1. Kennedy was murdered in November of 1963.

2. Kennedy was 43 when he was elected president and 46 when he was killed.

3. The Bay of Pigs incident occurred in 1961.

4. NATO, or the North Atlantic Treaty Organization, was in poor shape during Kennedy's administration.

5. The program for Latin America was called the Alliance for Progress.

6. Kennedy's plan for developing countries was called the Peace Corps.

7. Lyndon Johnson was Kennedy's successor.

8. Kennedy's successful domestic programs included (a) establishing the Peace Corps, (b) raising the minimum wage, (c) increasing Social Security benefits, and (d) getting more money for space programs.

9. The minimum wage is the smallest amount of money per hour that a person can be paid for work.

10. These bills prohibited school segregation and racial discrimination.

11. "Ask not what your country can do for you; ask what you can do for your country."

LECTURE 4
INDIRA GHANDI: A SAD SONG OF INDIA

1. Indira Gandhi's husband was Feroze Gandhi. Her father was Jawaharlal Nehru.

2. She attended Santiniketan University and Oxford Univeristy in England.

3. She was elected to Parliament in 1964.

4. She was found guilty of illegal election practices in 1975.

5. The party was called the Congress-I party.

6. Unemployment, food shortages and involvement in the Pakistani civil war caused unrest in India when Indira Gandhi took office.

7. Sikhs were not allowed to serve in the army, the state took away their water rights, national banks refused to invest in areas of India where many Sikhs lived and their holy shrine was defiled by government forces in 1984.

8. Two assassins participated in her murder.

9. Rajiv Gandhi succeeded his mother.

Unit 3
Ecology and the Environment: Natural and Human Disasters

Lecture 5
The Dust Bowl: Nature Against Humankind

1. Kansas was the state that suffered from such heat in 1936.

2. On July 24, 1936, the temperature in Kansas was 120 degress Farenheit.

3. These winds were called "black blizzards."

4. Overplowing and overgrazing damaged vegetation and topsoil in the Dust Bowl.

5. The first black blizzard was in November 1933.

6. The second storm hit Texas.

7. Dust Bowl counties lost 60 percent of their population to migration.

8. The farmers who left Oklahoma were called "Okies."

9. John Steinbeck's book is entitled *The Grapes of Wrath*.

Lecture 6
The Great Flood of 1993: Mother Nature on the Offensive

1. The word Mississippi means "Big River."

2. People also call the Mississippi "The Father of Rivers" and "The Big Muddy."

3. The Mississippi provided people with a convenient method for transporting goods and with water-powered electricity.

4. Minneapolis, Minnesota; St. Louis, Missouri; and New Orleans, Louisiana are all located on the banks of the Mississippi.

5. Papillion, Nebraska, received an inch of rain in six minutes.

6. When the river floods in the spring, the farmers can replant and still have crops to sell.

7. The Federal Emergency Management Agency helped flood victims.

8. The estimated cost of damage from the flood is $8 billion.

UNIT 4

CONTEMPORARY SOCIAL ISSUES: WOMEN, MEN, AND CHANGING ROLES

LECTURE 7
THE WOMEN'S MOVEMENT: FROM LIBERATION TO FEMINISM

1. The Women's Movement is a century and a half old.

2. Women were not allowed to inherit property, control money that they earned, have custody of their children in cases of divorce, or vote in elections.

3. Women in the U.S. gained the right to vote after World War I.

4. During World War II, many women began working outside of the home.

5. 1.5 percent of professional firefighters are women.

6. Women-owned businesses employed more people domestically than the Fortune 500 employs world-wide.

7. Ireland, Nicaragua, and the Philippines have had women presidents.

8. Barbara Ryan believes that the lack of government-sponsored child care is a major obstacle to women's emancipation.

9. Barbara Ryan's book is called *Feminism and the Women's Movement*.

LECTURE 8
THE MEN'S MOVEMENT: WHAT DOES IT MEAN TO BE A MAN?

1. Susan Faludi authored *Backlash: The Undeclared War Against American Women*.

2. Robert Bly is considered to be one of the Fathers of the Men's Movement.

3. Robert Bly's book is titled *Iron John*.

4. Some fathers of the Men's Movement blame the Industrial Revolution for today's crisis in masculinity.

5. Before the Civil War, most men were farmers, craftsmen, or shopkeepers, who worked close to their homes.

6. At the beginning of the twentieth century, many men became factory and office workers.

7. Men in the mytho-poetic Men's Movement believe men should be initiated into manhood.

8. This woman and her husband now share responsibility for their family's emotional well-being.

UNIT 5
INTERCULTURAL COMMUNICATION: THE INFLUENCE OF LANGUAGE, CULTURE, AND GENDER

LECTURE 9
CLASSROOM COMMUNICATION: LANGUAGE AND CULTURE IN THE CLASSROOM

1. Communication is talk, gestures or non-verbal signals that we use to send messages that convey our thoughts, emotions or intentions to other human beings.

2. Andersen and Powell's article is entitled "Intercultural Communication and the Classroom."

3. A ritual is a systematic procedure used to perform a certain act, or to communicate a certain message.

4. Students of Asian backgrounds generally believe they will learn best by absorbing knowledge given them by the teacher.

5. In Vietnam, classroom interaction is tightly controlled by the teacher.

6. The Vietnamese consider teachers to be honored members of society.

7. Students from Germany do not often disagree with a teacher.

LECTURE 10
GENDER AND COMMUNICATION: MALE-FEMALE CONVERSATION AS CROSS-CULTURAL COMMUNICATION

1. Gender is the social identity that men and women learn as they grow up in a culture.

2. Deborah Tannen wrote this book.

3. Boys usually play outdoors, have hierarchically structured games that are played in large groups. One boy usually acts as a leader, and the other boys try to gain status by taking "center stage." Boys games usually have clear winners and losers.

4. Girls usually play indoors, and in their games, everyone gets a turn, and the group makes up the rules together as they play. There are usually no winners and losers in girls' games.

5. The girls were making rings for their fingers.

6. In the game house, one girl usually acts as the mother. This girl gives orders to the girls who are acting as the children. In other girls' games, giving of orders is less common.

7. This stereotype is that women talk more than men. The research the lecturer quotes seems to disprove this stereotype.

8. A woman must paraphrase words sounding like the names of her father-in-law and brothers in Zulu culture.

Photo Credits

Notes